In Search of Mom

Journey of an Adoptee

Gallery of Diamonds Publishing

Costa Mesa, CA

In Search of Mom

Journey of an Adoptee

Michael Watson

Gallery of Diamonds Publishing

2915 Redhill Avenue, Suite G-102
Costa Mesa, CA 92626 U.S.A.

First Printing 1998 by KNI Incorporated.

Also by Michael Watson:

Why Mom Deserves a Diamond - 1,500 Essay Winners for 1998
Why Mom Deserves a Diamond - 1,002 Essay Winners for 1997
Why Mom Deserves a Diamond - 732 Essay Winners for 1996
Why Mom Deserves a Diamond - 391 Essay Winners for 1995
Why Mom Deserves a Diamond - 1994 Essay Winners
Why Mom Deserves a Diamond - 1993 Essay Winners

Library of Congress Catalog Card Number: 97-77982
ISBN 1-891665-29-4

Copies of *In Search of Mom* may be ordered directly from the publisher for $19.95 plus $3.50 for shipping (California residents add $1.55 sales tax.) For terms in volume quantities, please contact the publisher.

Acknowledgments

I would like to thank the many people that supported me in my quest. Whether biologically related or not, these persons shaped my personality and helped define my origin in the universe:

To my real Mom, Martha Velia Watson, the only mother I have ever known, the one who remained strong during my search, and the one whom I will always love immeasurably. In loving memory of my father, Stoy Watson. My beautiful wife, Maria del Carmen, who understood my compelling force. My daughters Adela Patricia and Michaela Maria.

My good friends Daniel and Sontaya, Brad, TJ, Slomo, Sandy, Maria, Terry and Anna. Also Tony, Randy, Bill, Don, Paula and Kim.

My *new* relatives Grandma Hattie, Uncle David, Aunt Joy, Aunt Mary Jane, Uncle Louie and cousin Michael. Also my siblings Michael David, Kenny Ray and Suzie. And Debra Kay, wherever you are.

Thanks to Celeste Brenn, Claudia Biesel, Daniel Roh, and Shannon Kirchoff for editing this book.

I would like to thank Helen Lotos and John Adams from the Orange County Public Library. Thanks to Suzie Singleton for her searching expertise, and journalist Tina Borgatta.

Special thanks to writer Dorothy Jean for following the Mother's Day contests since they began in 1993, and for editing this book. My deepest congratulations to all of the 14,356 students that have thus far contributed their Mother's Day poems and essays for me to read.

There are so many people who are responsible for the contents of this book. Please forgive me if you do not see your name listed.

Due to the compliance of our legal advice, a few names in this book have been changed. I sincerely apologize for those who would want their identities revealed, after all, that is one purpose of this book, to heal the plague, called Secrets, that is familiar to most adoptees.

I give dear thanks to the following authors for their extraordinary essays in this book. Listed in alphabetical order by last name: Kristen Adams, Brandi Andrews, Nakisa Aschitiani, Elaine Auyoung, Rose Avramescu, Falon Bahal, Jessica Barraco, Tina Basu, Amanda Bautista, Tawny Bayes, Joslin Beck, Lauren Marie Bielefeld, Seth Braithwaite, Shaun Brown, Ellen Chen, Tina Codini, Karin Coulter, Megan Darakjian, Sarah Demers, Kendra Dix, Jane Donahue, Ashlee Emmert, Nicole Esquer, Jennifer Field, Ayescha Gasdorf, Sheena Ghanbari, Candice Goldsmith, Lauren Grumet, Robert Hacker, Briana Haft, Nicholas Hangca, Dominique Hilsabeck, Leah Hollenbeck, Tammy Huang, Cassie Huger, Christina Irving, Ashley Jacobson, Stefanie Jednoralski, Jean Kanjanavaikoon, Margaret Ketchersid, Lauren Kiang, Scott Kircher, Jennifer Kissee, Amanda Lam, Jeremy LaMantia, Kristen Lara, Lauren Lavoie, Steve Lee, Chelsea Lindman, Dennis Liu, Emily Liu, Emily Looney, Tiffani Lynch, Natalie Maatouck, Lindsey Marino, Stacey McClurg, Jonathan McIntyre, Angela Mendez, Cindy Mescher, Tricia Michels, Amy Monin, Cory Morrow, Alison Murphy, Laurie Myers, Julianna Notti, Lauren M. O'Hara, Sinda Osburn, Emma Parker, Amanda Paugh, Danny Peart, Deborah Perez, Jimmy Pollard, Tony Qu, Andrea Quant, Omar Ramirez, Eric Reed, Katy Renish, Cristy Robinson, Rocio Rosales, Maricela Rubalcava, Michelle Ryan, Logan Saito, Robert Shenk, Genevieve Slunka, Lindsey Speegle, Katie Sporman, Jennifer Sutton, Michael Tan, Jason Daniel Thompson, Tina Toosky, Thuy Tran, Judy Tran, Ryan Underwood, Melissa Vadnais, Kaprice Vargas, Matt Walden, Meghan Watson, Rebecca Whitney Wright, Laura Wong, Katie Woodall, and Yana Yanovsky.

Preface

The life of an adoptee is sometimes like that of an ancient voyager who searches for the unknown. The explorers, however, used navigational tools and the stars to guide their destiny. They had their sights on the wonders that lay ahead of them. An adoptee, on the other hand, travels in the opposite direction.

The adoptee searches for the past. Therefore, he or she cannot rely on sophisticated equipment or the constellations, but rather hope and perseverance. The map of the past is many times derived from faint clues that one has heard or seen.

I am a prehistoric time traveler -- an astronaut of the past. I am adopted.

Perhaps we share the same circumstance. According to the most popular estimates there are currently six million adoptees (or one in fifty) in the United States.

I was born February 25, 1958. I saw my original birth certificate thirty-seven years later. The name was anti-climactic, simply stating "infant." I was an adult before I discovered that parents of adoptees are issued altered (or *amended*) birth certificates. Three days after my birth the name "infant" had been changed to the one I have owned ever since. All the traces of my ancestry were stripped away. I had no blood roots, and the branches of my family tree ascended into nothingness. Life before I was delivered from a womb never existed. There was never a molecule that was genetically connected to me or a face that resembled me.

My past had been deleted.

In changing only a couple of letters, *adoptee* becomes *amputee*. The definitions are amazingly similar, for each implies that a piece of an individual that was once inherent has been wholly dismembered.

The history of our forbears has woven a biological fabric through most of us. The foundation of the past has rendered a map to the future. This fabric is only an illusion to an adoptee, for the limbs of history have been severed.

In essence, my original identity died on 02/28/58, for an invisible hand had switched the blueprint for my life. The set of circumstances I was born into was forever changed. My adoptive parents, on the other hand, were given life, for I brought an immeasurable joy that was no different from the elation demonstrated by any biological parents.

In reality, by the laws of the court, I was *re*-born. Some adoptees have the sensation of a second birth. Others despair from being denied any birth. My original birth certificate and adoption proceedings became forever *sealed* in a tightly guarded file.

My life began when I was three days old. My proud adoptive mother can show you photos of me at that age. From that moment on I would travel through time at the same speed as anyone else.

But there would be no road behind me.

A newspaper reporter called this morning and said, "Are you the adopted child?" I suppose I answered correctly by saying yes, for I would be an *eternally* adopted child. Adoptees are not allowed to grow up.

As an adoptee, it is difficult to comprehend the feelings of an adoptive parent. Likewise, one can not pretend to experience the emotions of a birthparent who has relinquished a child. Every adoptee and adoption is unique, just as every reunion is unique. Therefore, it is not expected for the reader to have the exact hopes, fantasies and fears as the author.

The goal of this book is to enrich the reader by unveiling the emotions that forever possess many adoptees, like me, who have lived or continue to live in the world of ancestral bewilderment. I was careful not to conceal incidents that were tragic or otherwise painful at the time, and I chose to include them, feeling the honest renderings would give the book more strength. I hope these accounts will give inspiration for every reader and member of the adoptive triangle; which is the adoptee, the adoptive parents, and the biological parents.

Although this book is not a how-to manual to find someone, a searcher is invited to use any ideas herein for his or her own purposes. Every searcher will have a completely different set of circumstances and constantly changing levels of aspiration.

It would be intriguing to ascertain how an individual would differ if history could be changed; if one was given different surroundings and different adults to be reared by, if one was raised by biological parents instead of adopted ones, and vice versa. Although heredity is the main determinant of one's physical attributes, I am quite certain that my adopted parents and environment have shaped the thinking individual that I am today. My wonder and curiosity, along with my perception of love and life, is an absolute result of the experience that the daily process we call *living* has given me.

Some may say that they know an adoptee who has no desire to uncover his or her biological roots. From the many sources I have read, I am convinced that there is an underlying hunger in every adoptee, whether conscious or not, to know his or her origin in the cosmos. Some adoptees will take many years before they are psychologically ready to attempt the search. Others will never attempt. But I believe the yearning is still there, however dormant.

An adoptee's longing to find his or her roots should not be interpreted as a lack of devotion to the adoptive parents. In many cases, it is a psychological journey to find oneself. It takes emotional security for adoptive parents not to feel threatened, and incredible strength to actually offer support in the search. Many adoptees have recognized a stronger bond with their adoptive parents after reunions or contacts with birthparents.

I am one author who agrees that one's birthright should be an unconditional human gift. After learning the truth of their births, no matter what the circumstances, most adoptees have experienced an emotional release. The pages of the past reveal where one has been, and they are stepping stones to the present. And although I do not believe the past should dictate one's future, I do believe most humans have the extraordinary potential of seizing their individual destinies, no matter what set of conditions the world has rendered them.

A sociologist once said, "Unlike puppets, we have the possibility of stopping in our movements, looking up and perceiving the machinery by which we have been moved. In this act lies the first step toward freedom." Although the reference was about the difficulty of rising above one's current socially stratified state, I now see the words differently.

The puppets are those adoptees who live in the illusion that their adoptive parents are their "real" parents. They have symbolically erased their birthparents from their consciousness and have completely removed them from the map of their being. I am saddened by those adoptees who are afraid, for whatever reason, to inquire into the origination of their making, for they sometimes live in deliberate darkness during their entire lives.

The machinery is the probate court, the placing attorney, the physician at the time of birth, and the adoption agencies. It is the entire adoption system, from when the birthmother first signs the order of relinquishment to when the social worker makes periodic visits to the adoptive parent's home.

And finally, the freedom is the closure that the adoptee obtains from learning the most basic truth most of us take for granted -- our origin.

There will be uncounted adoptees who will never unravel the mystery of their ancestry. Other adoptees will never know their heritage simply because they refused to look for it. Still others may have an ardent passion but few clues to follow. However, it is our never-ending curiosity and the pursuit of knowledge that has been woven into us through the ages that has defined our humanness, and if the reader is currently searching, whether a birthparent, sibling, or adoptee, I wish you much success in your endeavors.

I will generally refer to the woman who gave birth to me as my *birthmother*. Other names I have heard are; *physical, blood, biological, original, true,* and *genetic*. I usually do not like *natural* because adoptive parents do not like to be regarded as *unnatural.*

Before age thirty-six I was dead, at least that is what my biological family had presumed until I proved otherwise. And although many horrors were uncovered during my search, that magical moment of reunion, on September 4, 1994, will forever echo joyously in my brain.

My investigation of the past began when I was seventeen, and I was terrified yet overjoyed at the grand finale of the twenty-year journey. It still makes me shudder to think how history would have been changed if I never questioned my roots, if my parents never told me the little information they were given, and if I had run away scared from failure.

On the following Tuesday afternoon I flew back to my home in Southern California. My mind resounded with inspiration. I began writing this book on the airplane.

Now I feel more alive than ever and am able to safely take the reader through this memoir in first person.

From here the reader is invited to travel with me through the pages of self discovery. I can only write from the experience of an adoptee, and I hope it will give a new understanding of the eternal hope for closure.

Perhaps the most important aspect about *In Search of Mom* is that it is a success story, and reveals that belief in oneself, blended with persistence, can move mountains.

Table of Contents

Acknowledgments 3
Preface 5

PART ONE -- The Journey

1. **Primal Beginnings** 15
   The Bed of the Truck 20
   Elementary School 22
   Where Did I Come From? 23
   Misery of Maturing 26
   Memories of High School 32
2. **First Search** 37
3. **First Love** 45
4. **The Registry** 49
5. **Harvest Homecoming** 51
6. **Second Search** 53
7. **Danger In The Snow** 57
8. **Good-bye, Angela** 61
9. **In Search Of Diamonds** 63
10. **Mountain To Heaven**
    Special Reading 71
11. **Mother's Day** 75
12. **Behind The Curtain Of Fear** 79
13. **Where Is Michael Watson's Family?** 93
14. **In Search Of California** 99
15. **Gallery Of Diamonds** 113

16. Lady By The Lake 117
17. The Mystery Clue 121
18. Journey To The Black Hole 129
19. The Reunion 141
20. Dad 147
21. Opening The Files 153
Epilogue 159
Photos 161

PART TWO -- Why Mom Deserves a Diamond Essay Contest

Special Reading 171
Past Diamond Winners 175
Outstanding Mother's Day Essay Winners 177

PART THREE -- Resources

National Search and Support Organizations 197
Social Welfare Organizations 198
Search and Support Groups by State 200
Canadian Agencies 206
Magazines 206
U. S. Government Agencies 206
Bibliography 209
Index 211
Order Form 215

PART ONE
The Journey

1. *Primal Beginnings*

Adopted was an abstract word in my early years, but it was a familiar sound not too long after *mommy* and *daddy*. I also have harnessed memories of Mom calling me her *little adopted angel.* I grew up knowing about my unusual circumstance and never really thought too much about it until I was a little older. Then I started asking questions such as, "You mean you're not my *real* Mom?"

During childhood, I felt somewhat special from my unique situation of being *chosen*. I remember Dad telling me that they picked me out from a large room filled with cribs of babies. After seeing me in the middle of the room, he said, "I'll take that curly-headed one over there!" Mom told me that before I was born her arms would ache with envy every time she would see a mother holding a baby.

For whatever reason, my parents could not have a child. They were told of a lawyer in Indianapolis that could bring them the hope of adoption. Years later they were notified from the lawyer and said that a baby would be born about the end of February that they could possibly adopt. Later they received a call saying that I was born, was a male, and they could come get me in three days. On the third day they drove one hundred miles to Indianapolis, signed the necessary papers, and returned south to the home that I would spend the next twenty-seven years of my life -- New Albany, Indiana. Dad was so pleased about his new son that midway he asked Mom to take over the wheel so he could look at me.

Several months before, Dad mumbled in his sleep, "Cr...Crit...Mi-kel Crit." (*Crit* was my grandpa's first name.) Mom heard the commotion and scrawled his words on a piece of paper. So hence became my complete name, Michael Crit Watson.

I lived in a three-story wooden frame house. New Albany had a population of about ten thousand and was a mostly a white Methodist town that was situated on the north bank of the Ohio River. Then it was basically a small village, looking across the river to its larger counterpart, Louisville, Kentucky.

I was the talk of the town and some confused neighbors exclaimed they didn't even know Mom was pregnant. Nevertheless, on that day, Mrs. Watson became a mother. By trial and error, she learned the correct amount of blankets to cover me and the safest way to secure my diaper with a pin. Never tasting mother's milk, I was given a stinky mixture that was synthesized from soybeans. I threw up regular milk.

My hair was extremely dark and curly, and I obviously didn't look like my fair-skinned, English-descent adoptive parents. My complexion was olive and I was labeled Italian-looking by friends and neighbors.

When I was two, Mom noticed that my feet would turn outward when I would lie on my back. The doctor prescribed braces that I would wear for the next two and a half years. The awkward contraption forced my feet into a "pigeon-toe" position. When I would crawl, she would always know where I was from the clunking sound.

Mom's name was Martha Velia. Somehow the nickname "Micky" stuck with close friends. And for whatever reason, Dad called her "Veeler," disfiguring her name even more. I always remembered her as plump, gracious, and quite attractive. Her most fascinating asset was her exceptional ability to gain the complete friendship and trust with anyone she would meet. She also had the uncanny ability to dissolve any argument between two persons with caring words and the wisdom of King Solomon. I always thought of her as an extreme worrier and tried to make her see the more serene side of life. She didn't quite graduate from high school and married Dad in 1944 when she was twenty-three and Dad was twenty-seven. She kept a spotless house, re-painted every room a different color once every two years, and hung clothes on a tight wire suspended between two mulberry trees in the back yard long after most neighbors had more efficient ways of drying garments.

Dad was a tall, thin man named Stoy. He finished only the seventh grade, entered the Civilian Conservation Corps in 1935, and worked long hours as a pipe fitter at DuPont until his retirement. He was always quite reserved unless some of his drinking buddies came over. Then, however, he could be quite intolerable if he had one too many gulps of Yellowstone. He had a hard life, and like many other people living in America during the Great Depression, was more concerned with economic survival than even the most primal luxuries.

His eyes were two different colors: blue and green. He lost fifty percent of his vision in one of them, I don't remember which, from being punctured with a tree branch while running through the woods as a youngster. He and Mom got along fine when he wasn't drinking. He smoked stinky smelling Tareyton's until his later life and then changed to a pipe. He was the only man I ever knew who could take a drag from a cigarette so deep that smoke would pour out of his mouth after the third exhale. The sun-filled living room was always infiltrated with horizontal layers of blue-gray smoke that would lie motionless across the living room unless a breeze came through.

Mom said she and Dad purchased our house in 1951 for eleven thousand dollars. Although it was built only seven years before I was born, I remember it as always being quite ancient. As an adult I now miss the nostalgic creak of its wooden floors, the oversized bathtub, and the panoramic view of mature maples and gentle hills from our back porch. I used the upstairs attic for dreaming and throwing darts at the crayon caricatures of monsters I had drawn on the cardboard walls. We rented the downstairs to various occupants who always seemed to make more damage than was justified by their monthly payments. The house was built on a sloping hill and the downstairs tenants had their own backyard access. My parents spent most of their lives on that middle layer.

We had a small farm thirty miles away. Dad was born there and was the recipient of the property after his mother died. On Saturdays we would drive our green Chevrolet truck there, spend the night, and return the next day. There was really nothing to do. Exploring the countryside, I would hurl dried dirt clogs against the trees, exploding them into rusty brown smoke. The muddy water of our undersized pond was a great place to wisp tadpoles with a glass jar. Mom would do most of the physical labor, such as unloading and loading the truck and cooking dinner. Dad would sit in a folding lawn chair in the back yard and drink beer.

The first negative encounter I remembered from being adopted was when I was about seven. A little girl who lived next door exclaimed in a hateful voice, "I know something you don't know...you're adopted!" Although that was a familiar word, I wasn't fond of the tone.

"So what?" I fired back.

"Your mom is not your real mother."

Lost for words, I scampered back up the hill to ask Mom what was so bad about being adopted. Noticing my confusion, she reassured me that adoption was not bad, but beautiful. She even gave me the correct comeback words to say if I was ever challenged with that question again.

The next day I saw the girl again. When she brought up the same subject, I had Mom's words memorized: "I might be adopted, but at least I was picked out special and your parents had to take what they could get!" The girl ran into her house crying. She never confronted me with that issue again.

I had invented a super hero, *Lizard Boy,* who would be the vigilante of the universe. Wearing Mom's green bath towel as a cape, I would dash down the hill with the garment fluttering behind me. I always dreamed of flying but could never become airborne.

Mom said I was christened at two years old. Ritually sprinkling a few drops of water onto my forehead, the minister paved my way into the Methodist denomination. Before we left, she would put a pot roast in the oven embellished with whole potatoes, carrots, and onions. When we returned from the service, I would savor the aroma as I entered the house.

Mom and I would always eat in the kitchen. She delivered Dad's dinner on an aluminum tray, and he would eat in the living room while watching television. In a blend between serious and playful, he would always refer to Mom's cooking as garbage. He had an acute sense of smell and cautiously sniffed everything before inserting it into his mouth.

"Veeler! Whar's my garbage?" he would protest from the living room sofa.

"I'm coming, Stoy, just hold yer horses!" she would yell from the kitchen. Mom would run to the rescue, spread Dad's dinner on the coffee table like a waitress in a fine restaurant, and return to the kitchen.

I always wondered why Mom was so subservient to my Dad, and theorized it was a mixture of respect and fear. Mainly the latter. Except Sundays, our supper menu never seemed to vary: pinto beans with a strip of jowl bacon, fried potatoes, and corn bread.

I have scant memories before age seven, and I do not believe I had any phobias beyond the darkness of night. However, I do remember one incident that almost eternally defined my fears. Once in bed, and from the light of the moon, I saw a giant wolf spider trample across my bedspread.

I screamed.

Mom came to my rescue, assuring me that it was gone and that I had probably scared it to death. In slow motion I relaxed my torso back onto the bed. With the covers pulled tight up to my neck, my eyes were wide open and I refrained from breathing for what seemed like several minutes. I was certain there was a "nest" of them nearby.

Then there he was again. But this time I could even feel the creature's weight as it raced across my chest. I yelped again, catapulting the covers as high as the ceiling light. Mom returned and this time we found it and annihilated it. That was it, I thought. I almost decided to fling my modest belongings over my shoulder and look for new real estate.

I treasured Saturday mornings. Homework took fifteen minutes the night before, and I pretended the weekend was a miniature vacation. I would lie belly down on the living room floor and watch cartoons as the sun poured brightly through the old wood-framed windows.

Mom would make biscuits and gravy. That was the only time Dad would ever eat with us. He broke the hot bread into small pieces, immersed it with white gravy Mom prepared from the drippings of fried bacon, then garnished it with black pepper. After we finished eating, we left for the country.

The Bed of the Truck

I used to ride in the bed of the truck while going to our small farm. I looked forward to the Play-Doh fragrance of wild roses which grew alongside the dusty gravel roads. If I was lucky, I would see a swarm of zebra swallowtails, a scene never observed on Grantline Road. Sometimes there would be as many as fifteen fluttering about a single bush. Swinging my badminton racquet until my arms were sore, I dreamed of swatting one then squishing its eternal beauty between two pieces of glass.

Of course, I hated the loathsome spiders. Inside the tilted outhouse, which I despised, was a place where I would always shake with terror wondering if a fanged creature would fall from the ceiling onto my back. The outhouse was also a favorite place for red wasps and mud daubers to build their nests. Going into the outhouse meant invading their privacy. I had to politely enter, shut the door ever so gently, do my business and leave.

I would sit on that hump in the bed of the truck, above the back tires, and the fresh country air would pound into my face and hair. Sometimes the aroma of cow manure or skunk spray would suddenly appear, and Mom would return a scrunched smile from the cab window.

I would lie on my back and gaze into the sky. The eight cylinders would rumble close to my ears and road bumps would rattle me to and fro. Before leaving the city, telephone wires and overhanging shaggy trees would zip over threateningly. Dad would make many right angle turns and the entire heavens would shift accordingly. Birds would appear to make a sudden yet choreographed about-face in the middle of the sky.

On the expressway my peripheral vision would consist only of fluffy white cumulus clouds floating on a gentle blue background. I could tell Dad would be driving fast from the engine's strained roar. But no matter how fast the truck sped the huge clouds would remain motionless in the sky.

The motor's clamor and the boundless sky had a mesmerizing effect. After several minutes of looking into the heavens, my brain would sometimes inform me that I was looking *down*! I sometimes became terror stricken, wondering what would happen if the earth's gravity suddenly reversed. I would fall directly into the clouds! Although the thought was absurd, the possibility was stronger than anyone could have convinced me otherwise.

My panic would temporarily dwindle as a bump by a stray stone assured that I was perfectly safe, lying in the cozy bed of Dad's truck. I would relax again and imagine falling back in time when the universe was created. When I was created. Then I would wonder about the little girl who said I was adopted. Did she know something that I didn't?

Then the outside wind would creep into the bed and whirl around and strike me with a terrific speed, perhaps a feeling similar to the air rushing up into a parachutist's face while descending from an airplane. But even higher. For I believed that every sky diver, no matter how high above the clouds, would be able to discern his destiny. But there was no destiny where I gazed.

With every expedition to the farm there would always be that moment when I would swing around and clutch the truck's edge, shivering with my face turned downwards. I was never able to look into the sky during any length of time without holding onto a secure object on either side of me. During those childhood voyages I could never seem to lie back and harness that higher level of consciousness. And, as an only child, I did a lot of dreaming in the back of that truck. I never once realized that my imagination would someday dispatch me on a twenty-year journey to find my beginnings.

At night time on the farm I slept in a small bed in the extra room. The ruffling oak leaves and the symphony of bullfrogs and crickets were never tranquil, but lonely. There wasn't the familiar swish of passing cars or the screaming of impatient fire engines like on Grantline Road. I had no brothers or sisters, and I was always aware of my solitude. I suppose one always fears what she cannot see, and when the lights were turned off, I shielded myself with the covers to ward off any spiders with a sense of humor that might drop from the ceiling.

Elementary School

I went to Fairmont until the sixth grade. In the beginning none of us were different from the other as far as being black or white, adopted or non-adopted, and we were all equal underneath the roof of that school. The teachers never seemed demanding or asked questions that dealt with equations or algebraic expressions. We did spend quality time listening to classical music while most of us put our heads on our desks and either fell asleep or just basked in the soothing sounds of Mozart and Vivaldi.

I do remember that precious time when life was as pure and simple as drawing with color crayons on manilla paper. Favorite compositions were various flying machines that propelled red and yellow flames. Pastoral scenes were green for grass and hills, blue for the sky, and an occasional house, horse or man which rested on the lower green level about one-quarter from the bottom.

Although I was not fortunate enough to have saved one of those masterpieces, I do believe my personal feelings were reflected in my human characters, who usually smiled in their frozen crayon states. I was left-handed. As a result, I always had graphite, paint, or different colors of permanent markers on the inside heel of my palm from smearing my artistic works with the very hand that created them.

I don't recollect listening to classical music or exploring with Crayola crayons in the later grade school years. Lunch time and recess seemed to be the only highlights of the day. Mom would assemble a sandwich with some cookies or potato sticks that I would carry in a brightly-colored lunch pail featuring popular comic book heroes. On the playground my favorite sports were kickball, square ball, and searching for interesting bugs underneath rocks.

Mom promptly picked me up after school and would wait in the parking lot with the other mothers. Standing alongside each other, I noticed the mothers appeared much younger than mine. One of them remarked as I came to the car, "What a fine boy you have, Mrs. Watson. Where does he get that lovely curly hair?"

Mom's face would beam during any compliment about her son. "He's adopted. We got him when he was three days old," she would say.

Although it was obvious to Mom that I was certainly special, it was perplexing to me. Later in life, I would wonder what I was so special about. Maybe "special" was a synonym for "rare." In that case I would be like a precious gemstone, something that everyone would admire.

Where Did I Come From?

Mom always had the remarkable ability to know when something was wrong, and sometimes I wondered if she could telepathically read my thoughts. Either I was thinking aloud or she noticed I was more quiet than usual, but she came in my bedroom and sat on my bed.

"Where did I *really* come from?" I asked. "Do you know who my *real* mother is?" Mom comforted me in her beautiful way by grabbing my hand and pulling me down beside her. She concluded for the hundredth time that she and Dad were my *real* parents because they picked me out specially.

At twelve going on thirteen, I didn't settle for that answer anymore.

"Where did I *come* from?" I demanded more seriously, stressing a different word. "Who was my *mother*?"

"Stoy, honey?" she projected her voice around the hallway. "Would you come in here for a minute?" The bedsprings cringed from our weight.

Dad's face appeared from around the corner. He had an unusually earnest expression from Mom's imploring tone. "Whaddaya want, Veeler?"

"Michael wants to know about his birthmother."

"Well, tell him." he said.

Both of them stared at each other for a few seconds waiting for the other to speak. Dad spoke first.

"Your mother's name was Betty Price. She was twenty-two years old when she had you, and you were born at Community Hospital in Indianapolis. That's all we know, Mi-kel. If we knew anymore, we would tell you, but's that's all we know." His voice was sincere with a shaky authority.

"Who was my father?" I continued, before completely absorbing the first answer.

"All it said on your birth certificate was, 'father unknown'. Maybe she didn't want to give his name... we'll never know," Dad answered. "And that's all we know, Mi-kel. All you need to know is that we love you more than anything in this world and that's all you need to know."

And with that final proclamation he returned to the living room.

I turned toward Mom again. Her expression was the same as when she told me about the birds and the bees. For many years the secret was "the birds *fly* and the bees *buzz*." Later, she proceeded to tell me the truth, in adult language, and the whole idea of creating babies from the coupling of genitals was nauseating.

"Michael, like we have always told you since you were old enough to hear, we adopted you when you were three days old. We wanted to have a baby so bad..." She paused, realizing she wasn't answering my original questions. "Just a minute." She got up, went to her bedroom, made some clanging sounds from an old tin box that her and Dad kept in their closet and returned with a handful of papers. "Here. You can have these, Michael," she said, handing me three flimsy legal documents with dirty blue covers.

I carefully unfolded the one on top. It was labeled: *Decree of Adoption.* It was typed on wrinkly, onion-skin paper and almost disintegrated in my small hands. I did an eyeball review of the parchment and realized that most words were foreign and unlike the reading assignments from school. Other than the legal jargon, I did see the name Betty Price typed in several blanks. The other two blue documents were titled, *Petition for Custody of Child* and *Order.* They seemed like the same thing but with Betty Price's name typed in different blanks.

My life-force drained as I sat dumbfounded. If Betty Price was my *real* mother, then who were these people, I wondered? The thought of being *chosen* was not special anymore. I just wanted to be regular. The abstract word, adopted, began to take on the form of an unearthly silhouette.

"Why did my mother give me up?" I asked bravely.

"Honey, maybe she couldn't afford to keep you. Maybe she was unmarried and didn't have enough money to support you."

My stomach ached. I became tormented whether adoption was good or bad. Should I have been ashamed or proud? I surely didn't feel that this was a fortunate circumstance, and I realized that being adopted meant that someone originally rejected me. For years to come, the condition of being adopted would no longer be a joy, but rather a scarlet "A" that would be stamped forever into my consciousness.

"We got you through a private attorney, Michael. His name was Raymond Grimes. He was an old man then. He probably isn't alive now. The doctor who delivered you was Dr. William Turner. He was an old man also. Here," she continued, handing me an crinkled postcard. "This is where you were born. I saved it for you."

The postcard was a photograph of Community Hospital. It was rather drab, with no trees surrounding the pale brick structure. Scribbled on the back was Mom's handwriting, 'Where Michael Crit was born.' I couldn't believe it. She must have planned on giving me these papers since the day I was born. She had waited until that special time -- today. Then she handed me another paper. It was the actual bill that my parents paid for my birthmother's three-day stay at the hospital. It said,

```
Community Hospital
Date:    Feb-27-1958
Patient:Betty Price
Age:     22
Address:2115 N. Delaware Street,
Indianapolis
```

The amount due was typed at the bottom, totaling a whopping $63.50. There was some new data: 2115 North Delaware Street. I fantasized about her still living there. What did she look like, I wondered?

"Did you ever see my mother?" I asked.

"I could have, I guess," she answered. "She was probably still in the recovery room when we went to get you. But she was the farthest thing from our minds, for it wasn't her that we wanted, it was *you*."

I felt like crying from the emotion and confusion, but I held it inside.

"We love you, Michael. You were the greatest thing that has ever happened to me and your daddy. Just because Betty Price gave birth to you doesn't make her your mother. I took care of you when you were sick, made you lunch every day for school, and put a Band-Aid on your knee every time you fell." She smiled, gave me an unusually tight hug, and went back to the kitchen.

I didn't ask any more questions.

Misery of Maturing

At thirteen I was initiated into the unbearable era of junior high. Just the thought of a different school frightened me. I would be plunged into an abyss of unknown students and teachers. I worried if I would be liked.

The following three years were the most confusing and a test of emotional stamina. Right and wrong blended together and were hardly ever complete opposites. I didn't know who to sit with at the cafeteria table, who to choose as a friend, or what was the answer to the problems of mankind. I also could never seem to determine my true character and realized there was no one I could turn to for that answer.

Although Mom still called me *special*, the word became like an old cliche. It had lost all former preconceptions I had of it every time it was uttered. My father was unknown. I was intelligent enough to discern that there was nothing *special* about being illegitimate. I agonized not knowing where I fit into this grand puzzle of life.

I was a bastard.

The joy I rendered to my adoptive parents must have been in direct proportion to the agony and despair I brought to my birthmother. Did I enrich my adoptive parents lives through the deprivation of my birthmother? Was I the pivotal point between someone's happiness and another's suffering? Was there a void in my parents' lives in which I was the cure?

I was a gift to my parents. But at the same time I was the sacrifice of my birthmother. I did not feel special anymore, in any sense of the word.

Hallucinations of my birthmother haunted me. Was she a beautiful princess or a whore? Was I the product of rape? Incest? Was I conceived from sacred love or lust? Was I a survivor? And if so, what did I survive? Did my birthmother die? And if so, should I mourn at her grave? Was she an alcoholic or drug addict? If I unknowingly married a sibling, *I* would be the perpetuator of incest. My dreadful imagination never evaporated into spoken words but remained sluggish in my brain. I never expressed any such feelings to Mom, and Dad was not the right person for such discussion.

During the eighth grade my voice dropped an octave. The hair on my legs started to turn dark. Later on my arms. A couple of black hairs sprang from my chest. I was transforming into a monster that had never before been witnessed by human eyes. I could not look to my father to determine my physical destiny, who was tall, with a smooth chest and thin blond hairs on his limbs.

My other nightmare was *losing* my hair. Dad used to take me to Ralph's barber shop as a child. One morning, as I was sitting behaved on the elevated swivel chair, old man Ralph made a comment that I have not yet forgotten, "Boy oh boy! Look at that thick, curly hair!" he exclaimed while snipping the back of my head. "I'll bet you'll go bald before you're thirty!"

Ralph must have predicted an accurate forecast, I concluded, for he had barber tools and paraphernalia all over the small shop, including four taxidermed deer heads protecting each wall like some ancient gargoyles. Since I was ten at that time, I calculated that my life would be over in just twenty more years.

Dad became more obsessed with drinking and would preach religious doctrine and yell at Mom. I would go to my room but the door would only muffle their commotion. He had a brother named Elmo who lived in the same old farmhouse where they were both raised. Dad claimed his father died when he was a child. His mother died of cancer. Later, Elmo was found frozen to death in the cow pasture. It was presumed that he had cut through the field to shorten his journey from a friend's house to his own, rested on a log and had a heart attack. My father wailed when he heard the news and never forgot about the way his brother died. A year prior DuPont had a terrific explosion in Louisville. The unexpected blast spun one little building around in a circle and twelve of his co-workers were killed.

I always felt sorry for the doom that seemed to gravitate toward my Dad. Rather than fastening onto happier reflections of his life, he chose to remember his misfortunes, which seemed to forever preserve his old age and melancholy.

As I got home from school, Mom would be watching the last episode of her favorite soap opera. Dad came home a little later with soiled khaki work clothes and the smell of Yellowstone on his breath. He always demanded his dinner to be brought to him on the coffee table from where he would watch the news. I guess he concluded that since he had worked so hard all his life he should be treated like a king in his home. I remember Mom making frequent trips to the living room while we were eating in the kitchen because Dad was grumbling about too much salt, not enough pepper, and so on.

As the evening advanced he would become more irritable. Sometimes my parents' voices would begin to drown out the television, and later the motors of passing cars. I had no reason not to believe that I was living in a typical American family and that all people had some sort of problems. Although I cried as a young boy, I learned that was ineffective after a period of time, and I would inevitably surrender to my room.

I was still going to church on occasion, and the members still affectionately remembered my recitation of l Corinthians Thirteen before the entire congregation when I was nine. I was supposed to have read that passage before the sermon, but instead I delivered the complete chapter from memory. Now I found myself rereading that chapter to find answers to my own turmoil. I had always felt I was conceived from the powers of the universe. Maybe I too, like Christ, was chosen to fulfill a divine mission. I carried a miniature Bible to school and preached to those who were destined to hell. I managed to find a meager audience but most were non-receptive and pretty heartless. I became better versed, however, and felt I could now have a reasonable conversation with Dad. I was wrong. After a month or so, I returned the little holy book back to Mom's dresser.

My classmates from grade school began to cultivate their own small groups. There were clusters of better academic students, those who flaunted their athletic prowess, and a crowd that just didn't seem to care about anything. I eventually chose to be with the latter, not feeling worthy enough to mingle with those I believed to belong to a higher social strata.

I started smoking, and although I was a minor I don't believe I was ever refused a pack by any store that sold them. I puffed in the morning on the way to school with my new friends, one on my way back from Jack's lunch house, and one on the way home. Eventually I even smoked in front of Dad. I don't remember him really objecting. Mom freaked out, of course. Steadily increasing my daily intake, I sometimes consumed as much as a half pack per day.

A sleeveless denim jacket emblazoned with a sew-on patch of Wyle E. Coyote, the never-victorious carnivore of the *Roadrunner* cartoon, was my attire for school. A hard pack of Marlboros would make a noticeable bulge in my buttoned, left front pocket. My hair was dark and thick and was especially popular with elderly ladies who would make affectionate compliments. My new clan let their hair grow down long. One guy wore it below his buttocks. Mine had the peculiar phenomenon of defying gravity: it grew straight up. Fortunately, afros came into vogue, at least in the negro community, and I was a forerunner of the fashion.

I acquired an outward toughness. Those with a brusque appearance seemed impenetrable and deviantly heroic, like the bad guys in comic strips that one really wants to see prevail. I also developed severe acne and a low self-image. When I received the proofs of my junior high class photograph I was so horrified with my portrait that I demanded not to be put into the yearbook. I was the only person in the entire school that refused insertion, and where my picture was supposed to be there was merely a black box with the caption, "Sorry, no photo."

I survived my first puff of marijuana at a rock concert, and although I didn't enjoy the euphoria, the pressure of being labeled a coward was too much for me. Afterwards, a joint always nestled in my Marlboro box. While walking to school one morning, I met with some other cigarette smokers underneath someone's carport. We would all take one large drag before going to homeroom. Later that day in Algebra class the principal came to the classroom and gruffed, "Michael Watson, please!" Everyone including the teacher turned to gawk at me. What did I do wrong, I wondered?

"Take me to your locker," he demanded.

I obeyed.

"Open your locker," he continued.

I made two nervous attempts at my combination dial. On the third try it opened.

"Remove your Marlboro pack," was his third order. How did he know about that, I thought. Then my mind raced.

Someone must have spotted my joint when we were gathered under the carport.

"Open the cigarette box."

I did.

"Take out the joint."

I did that too, and for years afterwards I would kick my butt for not shoving it down my throat to forever hide the evidence.

"Come with me to my office," was his final command.

Then he called Mom.

That was the most terrifying day of my life. Mom preached a sermon that I heard from her several times afterwards, "Michael," she said, "How could you do that? Why do you think we took you to church all these years?" *We,* she said. I don't remember *Dad* ever going to church. "Your life could be ruined because of this!" she continued deliriously.

Flashbacks of Dad telling me that I might have to go to a correctional institution haunted me. "They'll make you behave there," he would exclaim when he was drinking. He also told me a few times that they were going to give me back to the Indians. Being an adoptee, that pun was never funny.

"He's adopted. We got him when he was three days old," Mom said to the principal, almost apologetically. "We've always taught him right from wrong. I don't know why he would do this." Although I was convinced that being adopted had no connection with my aberrant behavior, I didn't interfere with Mom's less-than-scientific inference.

I sensed the end of my career as a junior high school student. Although frightened to death, I felt more sorry for Mom than myself. She loved me so much. I could see the disappointment in her eyes. She had already been through so much with Dad. Now, here I was, busted for drugs at the tender age of fourteen.

I pleaded guilty as charged, apologized to the judge, and was released on a misdemeanor. The whole ordeal made me angry because I never intended to ignite that joint anyhow. Nevertheless, I decided on my own accord to stay away from the chaos of weed.

As an adolescent adoptee, I never knew my potential as a human. Although no one in my immediate family had college degrees, I realized that it could be possible that my birthparents were geniuses. The school was sponsoring a spelling contest for the entire student body. I had a knack for English, so I channeled all of my energy into redeeming myself as a champion of this affair. The words given would be those from the vocabulary books of grades seven through nine.

Mom and relatives drilled me until I memorized every word. After becoming a finalist in my English class, the finalists then challenged each other in the auditorium. I don't remember being nervous in front of the hundreds of other students in their seats or my fifty rivals surrounding me on the stage. I had no fear of erring because I lived every word, and even though I had no idea of their definitions, I could clearly visualize the correctly spelled letters in my brain.

I came in first place, gave a quick bow to the audience and was awarded a chintzy pin-on emblem with a dingy yellow finish. The principal, who always seemed to have a close eye on me, seized my attention during the period break. He gazed at me with a phony smile, "Congratulations on the contest, Michael. Are you a smart feller or a fart smeller?" he said. Although it took me a while to understand his degrading humor, I didn't allow his remark to hinder my newfound self-esteem. And for the first time in my life since the innocence of my childhood, I was travelling again on the road in which the sign read:

I am important.
I am adopted.
I am the Chosen One.

Memories of High School

At fifteen the faces of classmates changed once again as I entered high school. Weary of carrying the weight of my curls, I cut them to a shorter but fashionable length. My acne began to clear. My cigarette habit dwindled.

Off and on, I had taken guitar lessons ever since I was seven. After so many years of Mom taking me to Woody's Music store,

I decided to do away with the sheet music and learn the remaining seventeen of the twenty-two frets.

I became adept with my electric guitar, and melodies that I felt were innovative Dad would proclaim as noise. The downstairs apartment had been vacant for years so Tommy Higgins, Greg Martin, Jesse Jenkins and myself coaxed my parents into using it to practice our instruments. After two hard weeks we had dreams of stardom. We launched a band called *Starrdust.*

At that time talent was equivalent to volume. Amplifier companies marketed total watts rather than tonal quality. Greg's bass would nearly rattle Mom's antique bottle decorations off the shelves upstairs and one time a painting fell off a wall. We got into trouble a lot with the shrill of the guitars and the bass frequencies that would pound into the neighborhood. The police came on several occasions but they would only bang on the downstairs door to get our attention, tell us to pipe down, and leave. We did some gigs at a few private parties but for the most part *Starrdust* was a legend that was only known by its four members. Grantline Road was no longer a peaceful and quiet place.

When the high school scheduled an entertainment show in the auditorium, I quickly fashioned a makeshift contract and booked the band for forty-five dollars. The band was introduced, the curtains opened, and *Starrdust* rocked two thousand watts into everyone's eardrums for fifteen minutes. We wore glitzy costumes and ran all over the stage. Greg jumped off of tall amplifier cabinets at choreographed times. Jesse's stage fright cemented him to the floor. I performed the lead solos on my knees. The students were just as awe-struck as ourselves. Half of them applauded. The other half were frozen in their seats with their mouths open.

Dividing the forty-five dollars as evenly as we could we were now paid professionals. My embarrassing former enigmas seemed to disappear and now I was the *guitar man.* Although the majority of students did not know my name, many would salute a thumbs-up when they would pass me in the hallways.

Upon becoming a legal driver, I spent Friday nights with my friends buzzing Frisch's Big Boy, a now-extinct car hop on Spring Street. Although too shy to initiate a conversation with the girls, most of the cruisers demonstrated their masculinity by revving up their engines, except my car, which was a blue '69 Biscayne. It was basically a miniature tank and never voyaged over fifty miles per hour when the accelerator was pressed to the floor. We inaugurated it the *Biscuit.* After ordering a cola, we would pour half of it onto the ground and refill the cup with sloe gin.

On one murky night we headed for the Knobs which was a terrain of hills that overlooked Louisville. On the way we came to a train crossing and Tommy shouted, "Ride the rails!" After I realized what he meant, I was caught in the peer pressure of driving on the railroad tracks. With much coaxing, I turned the *Biscuit* parallel to the tracks and hopped on. During the next five minutes my four-wheeled vessel took on the persona of the Santa Fe Chief. It was a bumpy ride and we could only go about fifteen miles per hour. Passengers of on-looking autos had never seen a blue train before. I sounded two long Beep-BEEEEP's and flashed my headlights from bright to dim. Jesse waved at spectators from the back.

We left the tracks and continued up the hill. Tommy Higgins could only talk about the girl that dumped him. Greg spilled sloe gin on his crotch. Jesse threw up out the window. The hill was snaky and cars had to drive slow because of the thick fog from the higher elevation.

"Your nose is bigger than your dad's," Greg jested to Tommy before I made an unexpected sharp turn.

"Get out of here, man!" Tommy fired back after we straightened our slanted positions. "At least my dad didn't give me a big strawberry nose like yours!"

"And where did you get that wild, kinky stuff on your head, Watson?" Jesse groaned from the back as the *Biscuit* descended steeply. "Oops. Forgot you're adopted."

"Look out!" Tommy screamed. I squinted my eyes and slammed my brakes. My vision was blurred. I didn't see that the road had suddenly made a right angle turn. We were heading over the cliff.

The sound of tires sliding from the misty pavement onto the wet soil was terrifying. A second later we hit a boulder. We swayed out of the car, then peered into the destiny that the boulder denied us. The ravine sank into oblivion. There was complete stillness as we looked at one another. Occupants of a nearby house must have heard the impact, for we could see the graduating silhouettes of a Dad-Mom-Teenager-Child behind their living room curtains, straining for a glimpse of the tragedy. Although the *Biscuit* had only suffered the loss of a halogen eye in the collision, Tommy, Greg, Jesse and myself survived without a scratch and were very thankful.

Adoptive parents are expected to be happy.
Adoptees are expected to be grateful.
Birthparents are expected to forget their loss.

Differences. June 1996. Referring to speech given by Sharon Kaplan entitled- The Seven Core Issues of Adoption.

2. *First Search*

The resolution to find my birthmother was at seventeen. I hungered to find out who she was and therefore who *I* was. Now was my chance, I thought, to find the identity of my origin. I was tired of telling people "I don't know" whenever asked about my nationality. "What are you, Michael? Jewish? Greek?" Then they would say, "What do you mean, *you don't know?* What is your mother?"

"I don't know that either." I would say defeated.

"Who is your father?" They always prodded further.

"I don't know," I would continue stupidly. "I was adopted. I really don't know who or what I am."

Then the same story would unfold that I have told a thousand times. So many people just didn't understand what it was like to not know your mother or father or brother or sister. I also never knew what it was like to write with my right hand, but that handicap never made me feel cheated like the denial of my birthright.

I had my driver's license now. I was free. I had safely kept the adoption records that Mom had given me as a child. The address rang in my head -- 2115 North Delaware. I must go there, I vowed to myself.

But what would I do after I arrived? What if my birthmother was still living there? What would I say, "Hi, Mom, I'm home?" Or could I ever address her with such a sacred title that I had only vocalized to the woman who nurtured me ever since I was seventy-two hours old? Then I thought of every conceivable danger associated with this sort of quest. What if she was married and never told her husband about me? What if she had other children? I could destroy her marriage and her life.

The fear of the adventure almost became too great for me. Mom was not prepared when I told her my decision. I really do not think she could understand why anyone would want to seek answers to such questions if they had wonderful adoptive parents.

I figured that maybe a letter, hand-written by me, would be a better solution to this dilemma. After much thought I wrote:

> Dear Mom,
>
> I know how you feel when I ask questions about being adopted. I'm not searching for a new set of parents. I just need to know where I came from. I've never met anybody who has ever resembled me, and sometimes I feel strange.
>
> I know you told me that it is the people that raise you that are your real parents, and you have cared for me more than most other mothers I have ever known. But I just want to know the truth.
>
> I'm driving to Indianapolis. Please don't worry. If I find my birthmother, please don't think that I'll forget about you. That could never happen. As far as I'm concerned, <u>you</u> are my mother.
>
> I don't know what I will find. I am a little bit afraid. I hope you understand.

The next morning I placed the note face up on the kitchen table and left before the sun had risen. The day before I had driven by a gift shop and purchased an inexpensive gold-plated amulet. It would be a token for my birthmother and symbolically mean that I did not hate her for relinquishing me. After all, she had given me the gift of life. The amulet had two graceful curves, representing her and myself. The larger curve seemed to "give birth" to the smaller one, which met each other at the bottom. If she would not want any further contact, then she could still keep the amulet as a reminder that I would be a part of her.

The outskirts of Indianapolis came into view at about seven a.m. Although the northbound drive on Highway 65 was formerly peaceful, I soon became tightly sandwiched between rushing vehicles. One hundred miles seemed like a terribly long distance to drive by oneself, especially after just receiving a license. As I jockeyed for space, I wondered if all the cars were beeping at me.

Miraculously finding the *North Delaware* sign, I slowly crept threw the calm street with large old houses and leafy trees on either side. It looked like a dilapidated neighborhood that was probably a nice place back in 1958. I saw 2111, 2113, and...nothing. There was no house at 2115! It was a vacant lot. I backed up to see if I missed something, but there was no such address. After curbing the *Biscuit,* I sauntered to where the house was supposed to be. The early morning air whisked by coolly on my bare arms. I saw only damp and warped wooden boards that lay criss-cross where a house used to be.

So this was the *Twilight Zone*, I thought, stomping around on the ground where my birthmother had once strolled. There was a mailman walking at a fast pace along the street. I stopped him and asked if he ever knew a Betty Price that used to live there. He replied, "I've been on this route for many years. Hmm... I think I remember a Betty Price, but it's been so long ago. Sorry, sir."

So off I went, trudging up and down the street knocking on every door. The first house was empty. The next occupant shuffled inside, then briefly peeked through the curtains but refused to answer. Another neighbor said they had just moved there two weeks prior and that they didn't know anybody. Then I went to the fourth house where an elderly lady answered. I told my story, and she departed inside to get her husband.

They must have felt my sincerity, for they escorted me to a dusty davenport patterned with large paisleys where I sat and sank halfway. The old man's forehead wrinkled, then he said he remembered a Betty Price that used to go bowling down the street every Wednesday night. He said that she walked with a limp, was short, and died in an auto accident many years ago. By the look on his face, I could tell he was struggling to assess his recollections. Somehow I resolved that he wasn't speaking about my birthmother.

After a few moments the man started crying, and when I asked what was the matter he composed himself and told this story:

"I once had a good friend who was adopted," he began, wiping a tear with a faded handkerchief that he fetched from his front pocket. "He didn't know that fact until he was about your age, when he found the documents between the pages of the family's old Bible. He became furious at his parents for not telling him, packed his belongings, and vowed never to return to his home again. But the biggest tragedy of all is when he found his real mother a few miles away."

"What happened?" I asked nervously.

"When she answered the door she said, 'I didn't want you when you were born,' his voice was broken and tears welled up in his eyes once again. '...and I don't want you now.'"

Jeez, I thought. Would I be strong enough to handle that ordeal? I felt sorry for the old man and his friend, but I couldn't relate that incident to myself. How could I be hurt by a woman whom I have never met? I also remembered my childhood friends asking me if I hated my mother for giving me up for adoption. Likewise, I would think, how could I hate someone that was only a hazy apparition in my brain?

I thanked both of them for their hospitality and said that I had to go to the city county building to see if someone would give me any more information. They invited me to return and said I could call every Price in the Indianapolis phone book if I wanted. I thanked them and left.

Arriving at the city county building, I was directed to the seventh floor where Probate Judge Jameson presided. I entered his office and was greeted by a balding, stout man who motioned for me from his large chair. I introduced myself, told him that I was adopted, and said I wanted to find my birthmother.

The judge paused for a few seconds to find the right words. "Adoptees come here all the time, Mr. Watson. They all want to know who their mothers are and where they came from." Then I swear it seemed that the judge held back a tear. I marveled why everyone was so emotional about my quest. After all, I felt that I maintained complete composure. "The books are closed, Michael," he continued. "All the records from your adoption are sealed. I'm very sorry. There's nothing I can do."

That was one of the biggest failures of my life. Before this encounter I had a clear vision of finding my birthmother on this very day. Now my dreams were starting to disintegrate.

The judge reached for a piece of scrap paper. "Maybe this agency can help," he said while scrawling an address. "Contact these people. They may be able to help you." He handed the barely legible name and address to me. I glanced at it dizzily, stuffed the paper in my pocket and left.

The elderly couple heartily greeted me when I returned to their house. The man gave a grandfather smile and handed me an already opened telephone directory. As I wearily gazed at the hundreds of Prices listed, I wished my last name had been Zarnowski.

I began to dial.

"Hello. My name is Michael Watson," I commenced. "The reason I am calling is because I was adopted here in Indianapolis, and I'm searching for my birthmother. Her name was Betty Price, and I was wondering if you have ever heard of her."

I received a different response every time. For the few numbers that didn't give busy signals or never picked up, most people were congenial. There were a couple of people who were pretty rude. One person thought I was a lunatic. Some would hang up on me. I always wondered if the latter knew the woman I was seeking or *was* the woman I was seeking but was frightened to say.

I didn't know anything about selling in those days, but I realized afterwards that that was my first education in telemarketing. For seven straight hours.

I also didn't realize how hungry I had become until the elderly lady asked if I wanted something to eat. When I gave her a positive answer, she disappointed me with a plate of lemon cookies and a glass of milk. Nevertheless, I devoured every cookie without leaving a crumb and continued calling between swallows and gulps.

The sky turned a shade grayer. The telephone was an old rotary style and its cumbersome weight was cemented to the Queen Anne table. If a number had a zero in it, the dial would take forever to spin back to its original position. The dial was stiff and my fingers became sore. For two hours I had been calling with no luck. Then the man and his wife reappeared with interlocking hands and said, "Michael, we are going to watch TV at our friend's house in Beech Grove. We're gonna find out who shot J.R. You can stay here calling as long as you like. Just be sure to lock the door when you go back to New Albany. "

I couldn't believe it. They were going to leave me there by myself. I was amazed how anyone would be that trustful of someone they had never met before. Then I remembered what they were talking about. That was the night that the world would find out who shot J.R. Ewing on the *Dallas* television series. While millions of Americans would be glued to their television sets, I would be glued to a telephone, calling every Price in the Indianapolis phone directory.

The couple left. I continued dialing. I became bored with my canned introduction and was quite frankly becoming tired of all the rejections and snub remarks. My stomach growled for food again, and I didn't want to raid the couple's refrigerator. From my chair I could see the kitchen night light reflecting off of bright yellow walls. Fantasizing about the delicious food hoarded somewhere in that kitchen, I began to salivate. The unwelcome illusion of lemon cookies entered my mind and made me sick. I needed *real* food. Taking two steps towards the kitchen I remembered the woman's words. "Keep on calling...lock the door." She did *not* give me the permission, however, to eat them out of house and home.

Marking my place in the phone book with a pencil I went outside, remembering to insert a thick piece of paper in the door jam so I wouldn't be locked out forever. I drove down North Delaware until I found a fast food chicken place. I made a hefty order and ate all of the unketchuped french fries before I made it back to the house. I accomplished a few more calls, dialing with a fresh finger. I smashed the empty chicken container in the trash can, licked my greasy thumb and went home. I left a nice thank-you note beside the telephone. This time I locked the door.

I returned to New Albany about eleven o'clock that night. Mom and Dad were waiting up for me. I have no doubt they watched *Dallas*. I didn't ask who shot J.R. Hardly ever watching television, I wouldn't have known the characters anyway. I told them that I didn't find anything or anybody, and that the judge would not tell me any information.

"See, Michael, we told you!" Mom spoke quickly and almost didn't let me finish my sentence. "They told us when we got you that the books are sealed. They cannot give out any information."

My soul was hollow as I shuffled to my bedroom, for I had returned empty handed. As I undressed, I found a now very crinkled paper that the judge had given me and tossed it beside my wind-up alarm clock. Then I dug deeper into my pockets and found a small box with crunched corners. The amulet. I removed it from its soft cotton bedding and momentarily observed its shiny gold reflection in my dim night light. I neatly returned it to a dark but safe corner of my dresser drawer and quickly fell to sleep.

3. *First Love*

Starrdust had alternated its members. Tommy Higgins a I stayed in the band. Greg left to get married. Jesse left to become a father.

There was a clubhouse in the Knobs that was known for its Saturday night dances. There were always great bands there that Tommy and I and other musicians would try to pick up pointers from. We also tried to pick up girls.

That's when I met Angela. She had long, dark hair and shapely curves. At semi arms length, she was revolving to a slow song with another young man. As soon as she dislodged her body from the boy, she accepted my offer to dance.

She was seventeen and even more beautiful as we resorted outside to the windless and humid balcony. Luna moths flittered by the incandescent lamps. After a few opening lines, she said she lived on a farm down the road where her parents grew produce.

"What do *you* do, Michael?" she asked. Now it was my turn to answer.

Other than playing the guitar, I was currently working part-time at a local bakery. My friends always jested that I rolled in the dough. The owner had the prestigious title of *Cake Decorator*. I, on the other hand, was the pan washer. Every day after school I would slave away by a monstrous dishwasher that held a load of thirty-five large pans. The owner would swirl *Happy Birthdays* in an air-conditioned room while I was sweating beside *Big Bertha*. Another short, hunched man who obviously spent his entire life there would roll semi-truck loads of dirty bakery pans smudged with a mixture of gooey cherry jelly, dried chocolate, and sticky glaze. He rolled. I washed.

"I play guitar in a rock band," I finally said, hoping that she would respond positively.

"Are you Iranian?" she asked without pause.

"No. Why?"

"Just wondered."

Then I explained, as convincingly as possible, that I was special because *no one* could figure out what I was. After more small talk we made our first date the following Saturday evening.

Her house stood remotely across a small ragged bridge. When I arrived, she was removing her trapped black cat from the ceiling of the porch. I offered assistance, and she asked me to catch the feline while she released it to the floor below. The fat animal was making low, gurgling sounds that sounded like a cross between fear and irritation. Although it was getting dark, I could see the white claws fully extended from each paw.

"Please don't miss my kitty when I drop him," she implored. On a first date I felt it was important to demonstrate heroism. It would be an honorable thing to do, to help this damsel in distress. On the other hand, I beheld the peril that lingered over my head as I peered up at twenty razor sharp knives.

I saw the pleading look on Angela's face. "Fire away," I said, squinting my eyes with my arms over my head more for protection than anything else. The frightened cat plummeted towards me. It adhered itself to my head. With my eyes still closed I grabbed the beast on both sides of its chest. Then the law of gravity took over. The animal dragged its claws from my scalp and slowly ripped me into twenty pieces as it descended to the ground with a moderate thump.

"You dropped my kitty," Angela said with disappointment in her voice as I was bleeding to death.

"No. I caught him. He's just fine...landed on all fours," I responded redeemingly.

I still do not recall what it was about Angela that captured my heart. Although our youthful minds were usually light years apart, she seemed to be the first person that understood my desire to find my biological origins.

4. *The Registry*

I found the wrinkled paper that Judge Jameson had given me a few weeks ago. It read, "A.L.M.A." and gave a New York address. The anacronym stood for Adoptees Liberty Movement Association. The judge had told me that this organization was helpful for adoptees searching for their birthparents.

After making a letter inquiry I received a form letter professing to put my name and birth date in its files for a thirty-five dollar membership fee. If my birthmother would do the same, a *match* would occur.

Sending the money was like betting on a Kentucky Derby horse. What if my birthmother never filled out the same form? Did she even have thirty-five dollars to send? Was she even still alive? Nevertheless, I eagerly filled out as many blanks as I knew the answers to.

I had never heard of an organization that was on my side as an adoptee. It was certainly not a topic that was brought up during casual conversation with my adoptive parents or my aunts and uncles. Actually, other than myself, I barely even knew anyone else who was adopted.

Above *Mother's first name* I wrote Betty. I was sure of that. For *Maiden name* I wrote Price, but wondered if that could have been her married name instead. When I came to *Father's name,* I felt nauseous from my ignorance and curled a bold question mark.

After returning the form with a money order, I received a fifty-six page booklet entitled, *Official Alma Searcher's Guide for Adults*. The organization was founded three years earlier by Florence Fisher and offered mutual support for adoptees. The marginless publication was crammed with hard to read print yet quickly confirmed that I was not the only adoptee concerned with his origination. A mosaic of smiling adoptees reunited with their biological relatives gleamed from the brochure, and I dreamily transported myself into the pictures.

Trudging through the booklet was painfully solitary, for I didn't feel there was an adult I could turn to for help. Nonetheless, after braving my way through the pages, I was confident that I would discover a way to contact my birthmother. She would probably be married, or remarried, and I imagined having sisters and brothers. She would be glad about finding me and knowing that I was alright. My mind happily branched into many tangents pondering the possibilities.

I waited and waited. Other than receiving a couple more newsletters about recent matches and reunions, there was nothing for me and nothing about my birthmother.

5. *Harvest Homecoming*

I remember the glory of Autumn. That was a season one could actually smell in southern Indiana. Light rain would dampen the already fallen leaves and the aroma would rejuvenate the senses.

The crisp air would gently massage one's face. The annual Harvest Homecoming would commence and the participants would range from toddlers to the old timers who molded the charisma of New Albany.

Residents would walk for blocks carrying folded lounge chairs, aligning themselves tightly along the street in preparation for the opening parade. Colorful floats, high school marching bands, and the Kiwanis mini-bike rodeo would cavort down the street. Clowns would throw handfuls of bubble gum into the crowds and children would scramble for it. The following day would render food and game booths all the way up and down Pearl and Market Streets. Vendors would sell candied apples, cider and homemade chocolate fudge. The thick smoke from the Bar-B-Qued chicken stands never bothered the glass blowers, who continued to spin delicate animal caricatures and merry-go-rounds.

When I was ten, the activity began as a mere pumpkin show, organized by the city's Chamber of Commerce with a humble budget of one hundred and fifty dollars. Years later it became the largest public attraction in the state, second only to the Indianapolis 500. Memories of Harvest Homecoming meant the thrill of being terrified at the Haunted House, taste testing pies, beholding humongous pumpkins grown by proud farmers, and being with your sweetheart. I took Angela.

Although *Starrdust* had sadly perished, I will never forget our last performance on the stage that was erected in the American Bank parking lot. However, I now recall that our forty-five minute concert began at ten on that Saturday morning, long before the more appreciative younger crowd had gotten out of bed.

6. *Second Search*

In 1977 I turned nineteen. Mother's Day and my birthday were always the days that triggered thoughts of my early existence. On Mother's Day I bought a nice card for Mom. I never bought flowers because Grantline United Methodist gave the mothers a small pot of marigolds. But I also thought about my other Mom. After all, she was the one who gave me life. I could have been abandoned on someone's front porch, aborted, or tied in a plastic bag and tossed into a dumpster.

My birthday was the other time that would reawaken the personal quest that slumbered in my soul. Surely that date evoked thoughts from my birthmother -- like those nine months, when I kicked violently in her womb during the last throes of pregnancy, ripping her insides out when I was born. Surely she remembered those agonizing pains of labor nineteen years ago. There must have been times when she saw a boy resembling her and wondered, "Is he my son?" Maybe she had February 25 marked on her calendar, imagining me grow one year at a time. She had to wonder what I looked liked, if I was alright, and what I would be doing at the present.

The worn, wrinkled pages of the Bible crackled as Mom turned each one from her chair. I wondered what religion I would have been taught under the roof of my birthparent's house. The sacred book from one family's coffee table could be the other's Koran. My physical features were Mediterranean, therefore it was possible that I could have been Muslim or Jewish. Although it seemed that the world was indifferent to such deep thought as why it could not possess a single belief system, I constantly battered myself with such theological questions.

Even though I loved my adoptive parents, there were many times that I felt that I did not belong in the grand picture. Although I was free to do what I wanted, I also felt trapped in an impenetrable glass sphere. Up until this point the sphere was my three-story house on Grantline Road.

One time Dad was bickering with Mom about the dinner that didn't meet his quality specifications. I walked into the front yard, then down the hill to view my home from a broader perspective. The diary of my childhood unfolded as I peered into the sphere. I imagined my puerile body running with the green towel behind my neck. Then I remembered Mom holding a glass jar in one hand and a hole-punched lid in the other as I inserted lightning bugs. I visualized me, Mom, and Dad waiting on the front porch greeting Aunt Arlie and Uncle Henry as they pulled into our driveway all the way from Dayton.

I was filled with a sort of reverence. I was grateful to have two parents who cared for me, who *rescued* me from the possible terrors of the past. Betty Price was the heroine for giving me the gift of life. My parents, on the other hand, were the heroes who *sustained* my life.

I scheduled a second odyssey to Indianapolis. When I told Mom she hurled the same, "But they said they could not give you any information!" It was always difficult for me to accept no for an answer. I softened Mom's worries with a kiss yet repeated the journey.

This time I had a plan.

The parking lot of Community Hospital devoured the *Biscuit* like an oversized monster. The enormous building didn't look anything like the meek photo of the postcard Mom had given me years ago. I asked for the manager in the records division and told him my request.

"My name is Michael Price," I changed my name. "I was born in this hospital on Tuesday, February 25, 1958. My mother's name was Betty Price. I need to see her medical records. She died, and I need to know if there is any hereditary illnesses that I need to be aware of."

I was certain the word "adopted" was taboo at the hospital. However, it was unnecessary to use that word because all the employees briefly looked up to see the poor soul who was searching for his mother and returned their heads to their previous positions. Then they looked at each other shaking their heads.

"I'm sorry, sir. We cannot show you that information," the records manager said.

"I even know the doctor who delivered me...Dr. Turner. Surely you have records..."

"I'm sorry, sir." I seethed from everyone calling me "sir" right before they gave me a negative answer. "Medical records are personal and confidential."

"Look," I pleaded, this time raising my voice. "What if there was cancer or diabetes in her family? Don't I have a right to know that? I'm nineteen. I am an adult. I have a right to know *where I came from*!" Whoops. Unfortunately, my mouth was traveling at the same speed as my brain.

"We're very sorry," resounded the broken record. "We cannot release any data here."

Then, from out of nowhere, a subliminal message crept into my mind, perhaps from the pages of the ALMA workbook. "Can you please show me the written law that says I am not allowed to know information about my birthmother?"

Same answer.

I stormed down the long hall. Then I saw something by the information booth that brought me to a halt: a rack of postcards. This must have been where Mom bought the postcard when I was born, I thought. The pictures were different, however, and one card showed the same frontal view of the hospital but was shrouded on the edges by giant trees. The hospital appeared to be at least four times larger than it was depicted in 1958. I made the quick observation of being unnoticed and pocketed one for a souvenir.

I returned to North Delaware and saw the same vacant lot. No one answered as I knocked on the elderly couple's door. Perhaps they had died. A hideous spider had built a thick web that connected the front door to its frame. It was obviously the new occupant.

Then I drove back to the city county building, and the elevator lifted me again to the familiar seventh floor. The judge was the same but seemed to have less hair. I wasn't sure if he recognized me, but after I repeated my request from two years earlier, he returned with the same negative answer, this time with a more profound finality.

I went home. My plan had failed. There were records in those archaic edifices that were rich in detail about my birthmother. About why she had to give me up, about who my father was, about my brothers and sisters. They knew who she was, but they would not tell me.

I arrived home a few minutes before midnight. Mom and Dad were still waiting up. I didn't feel like answering any questions so I went straight to bed.

7. *Danger In The Snow*

May the reader bear with me as I narrate this story, for this incident returned to haunt me as I neared the end of my search.

Other than a brief period of adolescent imprudence, I basically lived a sheltered life. But I was not a stranger to death. As a child I remembered all the funerals I attended. Eight, nine, ten, eleven. I would stand beside Mom at the coffin of the particular deceased and hear her remark how peaceful and nice he or she looked. One time I saw her give a quick kiss on the forehead to a corpse. Another time I forced myself to touch the hand of one of the doomed. It was cold and rigid.

The faces of the dead appeared before me. Although none were genetically connected to me, I had nevertheless addressed them with the prefixes of aunt, uncle, grandpa, and grandma. I never physically resembled any one of them.

I had already escaped death once, no twice. Other than the calamity on the Knobs, I remember once driving a little too fast on the bald tires of the *Biscuit* on a rainy afternoon on Grantline Road. The car suddenly made three full revolutions in the middle of the street. For a split second it seemed that my car was completely stationary, and it was the world that was spinning around me. When the twirling ceased I was facing the correct direction like nothing had happened. The cars ahead waited patiently for me to start my now stalled auto and I drove away.

I believed in the Destiny of Things. If it was my turn to leave the earth, then that fate should not be questioned. I shouldn't have been afraid of such an insignificant thing as death.

But I was.

Mom had just ripped away the month of January from the kitchen calendar. As intensely as spring reminded me of sprouting Easter tulips, the fragrance of southern Indiana air and immortal youth; winter made me think of death. The cold wind and snow gave no mercy to human beings. The news told everyone to stay off the roads except for dire emergencies. The weather had become treacherous, and all the schools were closed. I could understand how residents could be awed by the uncontrollable beauty that would blanket the earth and trees, but at the same time I was always perplexed how a person would desire to live in this perilous cold for several months waiting for the warmth of spring.

It was Saturday, the day I always drove to Angela's house. Mom and Dad told me not to go. I wasn't going to let the weather dictate my actions. So I left for her house with only a wind breaker and light gloves and kept warm mostly from the heater of a banana-colored Camaro Dad helped me buy. I drove carefully, for it had become almost impossible to go around a curve without sliding off the road. I took the new highway and exited the country road that led to Angela's house.

Featheringill Road was like a snake that writhed left, right, up, and down. About a mile from Angela's home, I descended what was to be my last hill. Driving no more than thirty five miles per hour, I saw there was no more road in front of me, but only a field of snow. As I applied easy pressure to my brake, the car slid into a silent oblivion of whiteness. I impacted into a four-foot drift. I tried to back up, but the Camaro's wheels spun hopelessly in reverse.

The arm of the gasoline gauge lay in that small red area just under the 'E'. I resolved to remain in the warm car while I organized my thoughts. I couldn't stay there forever, I calculated.

Then I wondered what would be the reaction of an astronaut if he casually noticed that his oxygen tank said zero. I knew no one would detect my dangerous dilemma because no one would be as dauntless as me to travel on Featheringill's icy road. I blew warm air into my clenched gloves, turned off the engine, and set off on foot.

The wind pierced my wind breaker like a scalpel. Breathing made me dizzy and I covered my mouth and nose with my gloves. The snow was deep and I became tired after only a few steps. The wind rang through my ears, and I found it impossible to cover my nose, mouth, and ears at the same time. Something would have to be exposed: my right ear.

In the blurry distance was an old house. I prayed that someone would be there and let me inside. Trudging through the thick whiteness, the apparition became larger and larger. My tennis shoes had become wet from the moist snow, and my feet began to burn. I couldn't feel my toes. I immediately remembered my Uncle Elmo who froze to death. Dear God, I thought, I was going to meet the same doom as my father's brother.

Nearing the old house I discovered that it wasn't a house after all, but an abandoned shack. Breathing became increasingly difficult because the freezing air would enter my lungs and make me cough. My ears and nose began to burn, and my balance was poor because I could not feel my feet. I fell twice. I turned back and could no longer see the yellow car. My mind raced. Something told me that going back would mean sure death, so I continued in the same direction, silently pleading that someone lived on that road.

I switched hands to relieve the burning from my right ear. The pain was real although my ear was numb. I had to breathe, but the freezing air would turn the wetness of my mucous membranes into instant ice. My mind was filled with horror thinking about the terrible death my uncle experienced.

I saw another house in the distance and forged blindly toward it. I started to cry. The wind showed no compassion and attacked the moistness of my eyeballs.

When I came to the house, I knocked and a middle-aged lady answered. My intended sentence was, "May I please come inside because my car wrecked and I am freezing to death?" What actually came out was a one-syllable, "Mmnsd!"

My mouth was frozen. There was no feeling in my lips. I immediately used my hands to wipe my mouth as if I had spaghetti sauce on it and rubbed it to cause friction. I imagined her thinking I escaped from a mental hospital.

"M-may I c-come n-nside?" My request was more understandable.

"Just a minute," she said. "Let me ask my husband."

Then she shut the door. I waited, still rubbing my lips in case I had to speak more. Each second went by painfully slow. One minute passed. Then two. I thought of the possibility of her not returning. I thought about Uncle Elmo. Maybe her husband told her to ignore me. Maybe she really didn't have a husband and was frightened of me. Maybe...

"Alright. Come in." the lady said standing between the halfway opened door. I stumbled inside.

It took several minutes to feel normal again as I quivered above the heater vent. I called Angela and her brother finally rescued me with his John Deere.

I stayed at Angela's house the next two nights until the wind ceased and the sun melted the ice from the back roads. Her parents obliged me with the guest room, complete with a crackling wood stove. I stayed awake late both nights, giving silent thanks for being alive.

8. *Good-bye, Angela*

Angela turned nineteen, graduated from high school, and became a part-time realtor. Her presence would energize my heart. Every time I saw a green '67 Mustang drive by I wondered if it was she. In fact, everything reminded me of Angela; when the phone would ring, when a love song would play on the radio, and when I saw her name that I had swirled in all my college books.

Angela was strong in her moral convictions. She also vowed to remain a virgin until married. I hardly ever encountered such remarkable willpower. Her body was firm and robust. I remembered when we fled to my room and reclined on the bed. Sometimes we would find each other's lips with closed eyes, embracing tightly yet fully clothed. Mom would purposely make loud shuffling sounds as she walked back and forth outside. In the course of thirty minutes, she would open the door at least three times as if she forgot to say something or because she thought she left something in the room. None of the bedrooms had locks.

Our romance had endured nearly two years, and though the reader may question my words, I only dreamed of seeing Angela in an intimate way.

I suppose Angela and I loved one another as much as humans are capable of, but sometimes our personalities collided. Other than a mutual understanding about the need to know one's biological roots, we seemed to have a solid but opposite opinion on almost every issue and claiming victory seemed more of a goal than getting along with one another. As time advanced there would hardly be a subject in which we would have the same consensus. Many ordinary conversations would loom into a fight. On one occasion we swung the bedroom door open with such force that its knob pierced the adjoining wall. Mom had to fill the hole with plaster of paris and repaint it. I thought of the hardships of my parents. They had problems. So did Angela and I. Sometimes I concluded that was just the way life was supposed to be.

Nevertheless, I told Angela I wasn't going to see her anymore. Although that decision was painful, I couldn't stand the anguish caused by our foolish bursts of outrage.

I dreamed about her for years afterward. We remained celibate, and because she so permeated my entire being, she forever drifted in my subconscious.

9. *In Search Of Diamonds*

Draped in black robes, the Class of '80 received their diplomas. After four years, I had earned a degree in business. Mom gave me a kiss. Dad grumbled about me selling my guitar and finding a *real* job.

Throughout the years, Dad always referred to my daily guitar practice as "that damn racket." I remember old man Slavo and his sidekick Tregger coming to our house one night when I was a child. Slavo sang and played a dented Sears Silvertone guitar as toothless Tregger slid a tubular metal object on the strings of his steel guitar. The music sounded out of tune even to my juvenile ears, but Dad still stuffed a twenty dollar bill into each of their pockets and exclaimed that was the best damn country music he had ever heard.

A year later I filled out an application from my university's job placement division. A couple of weeks later I received a call from the college informing me that Shalaars diamond company needed a management trainee. I boldly asked how much the job paid and they said two hundred dollars a week.

In 1981, two hundred dollars was not an incredibly high beginning salary for a college graduate. Anyway, I really didn't want to sell anything, for I dreamed of becoming a professional musician. I did need a higher income, and I was certainly not becoming rich from a guitar instruction course I had developed in the downstairs apartment for aspiring musicians. I agreed to set up an interview.

When I hung up the phone, I re-examined my talents: I failed miserably in accounting. I abhorred facts, figures, and wearing polyester suits. I wanted the autonomy of waking up when I wanted and writing memorable songs that would be hummed long after I was gone.

But I needed more money.

I walked over and straightened my college diploma hanging on the wall and blew off the top layer of dust.

For my interview the following week I wore my blue suit, the only one I possessed, with the final trimming of a red, white, and blue striped tie Dad had given me that clamped onto my shirt collar. My resume was skimpy, and I didn't want to revel about working in a bakery. So I made the connection that my experience from guitar instruction would be useful for Shalaars and that I did indeed work at Zemartan's jewelry store as a college freshman. I failed to say, however, that my duties were sweeping the floor and delivering repairs in the boss's run-down Gremlin.

The manager wore a drab brown suit with a stiff white collar that prevented him from turning his head very far. He directed his arms towards the jewelry showcases saying, "The public has a fantasy about diamonds. Some even think that when they see one for the first time it will burst into sparkles before their eyes." Then he shifted to a lower gear. "Anyway, one of our salesmen quit and we need someone else. Does this sound like something you would like to do?"

"I..."

"...of course, we really don't know if you can sell, but we could give you a try. You will also need to spend some time on the phone touching base with our old customers. "

"Yeah, I mean, YES, SIR!" I said. From seven hours of calling every Price in the Indianapolis phone book, I felt I had a head start in the telemarketing department.

I was given a "pre-employment examination" whereas I was asked a myriad of personal questions such as, 'Have you ever smoked marijuana? ...taken drugs? ...stolen anything? ...written a bad check?' Humbly confessing that I was ousted for pot in junior high, the manager gave a half smile and said, "When applicants say they have *never* touched pot, I figure they *must* be lying. Honesty is in utmost regards in this business, Mr. Watson. Please understand that we ask these personal questions because we want to make sure we hire trustworthy individuals."

I began to feel intimidated. The manager then said that all employees were "highly encouraged" to take a polygraph. Suddenly my mind flashed about two blue vinyl chairs with aluminum legs that I had taken from my English class in college. I somehow wanted to give credence to my guitar instruction course and thought a modern touch would do the trick. It was the only thing I had ever remembered taking that did not belong to me. When I met Mom at the front door with the bulky fixtures, I crossed my only two available fingers behind my back and told her I bought them at a yard sale.

The jewelry career that I had yet to begin had already ended. What could I say, I wondered? The needle would probably explode off the polygraph machine's printout if I told them I premeditated that heist for three months.

"So what do you say we start you off at two hundred dollars a week, Mr. Watson?" The manager said.

This was the grand finale. Realizing an unplanned need to negotiate, my mind searched for words and I said, "That's great! Of course that is two hundred dollars a week free and clear?"

The manager's smile relaxed. "Well, of course we have to take taxes out from that amount."

"Oh, I'm sorry, I misunderstood you. You see, with my degree I feel that I will command at least two fifty a week," I bit my lip and put my head down in contemplation.

"Just a minute," the manager finally said. "Let me talk to the supervisor and see what he says."

The manager retreated to a secluded corner and whispered into the supervisor's ear. Maybe I was too bold, I thought. I had never sold jewelry before. Neither had I sold used cars or real estate or cookies for grade school.

Then I worried about the blue chairs again. Getting the job was one anxiety, passing the polygraph was another. What would I say to the polygrapher?

The manager returned, "Alright, Mr. Watson. Since you had some jewelry experience at Zemartans, the supervisor agreed to start you off at two thirty-five. You should bring home around two hundred net."

Then I thought, Zemartans. That was the hot spot. I realized that Zemartans was a rival, and Shalaars would probably receive satisfaction in feeling that they intercepted an employee from their competition.

My employment would commence on September 15, of course, as long as the polygraph results were okay. We exchanged a firm handshake, and I left. I wasn't even excited about the job until I realized that there was a chance I would not get it. Now I wanted to prove myself. The polygraph was scheduled for the following week.

Returning home, Dad muttered that it was time I started looking for someplace else to live. I guess he was right, I thought. Some kids get evicted from their homes as soon as they finish high school. And many of those can't find jobs, get into trouble with the law, and beat up their wives, I continued to ponder. Mom said that I should continue to live at home and that I was not hurting anything.

I tried to change the subject by telling Dad I had landed a great job. Then he mumbled a cliche that I heard many times afterwards, "That job and a dime won't buy you a cup of coffee."

I worried every day before the polygraph examination. I was still giving lessons on those blue chairs for the past two years. I visualized my polygraph appointment. "Yes, Sir," I imagined saying. "I *did* steal two chairs from my university, but I promise I will never do that again."

My stomach twisted the day before the appointment. Then I could no longer bear the tension. I crammed the chairs into the back of the old banana-colored Camaro and returned to the college. I hauled the chairs back to the English building and into the same vacant class I had seized them.

I cleared my conscience. My criminal record was now pristine. I had never stolen anything, I justified to myself, but merely *borrowed* those chairs for two years.

The next morning I went to the polygrapher. He was a small-framed man that appeared to be in his fifties. He wore a detective-type hat and had small, beady, red eyes. I remembered friends suggesting that I hire an investigator, like this man, to find my birthmother, but I would always fervently refuse.

"Here you go, Mr. Watson." he said, strapping the instruments to my chest and fingers. "I will ask you some normal questions to get started. There's no need to worry about anything. Just relax."

Right, relax. I wondered if *he* had ever been subjected to such a dehumanizing contraption. The polygraph machine looked like some paraphernalia from two decades ago.

"Okay. We're ready!" His voice rose to a more enthusiastic level. "Is your name Michael Watson?"

"What?"

"Just answer yes or no please."

"Y..yes."

The polygraph machine whirred, then I noticed it marking black zig zags on the paper that slowly poured from it . "Please look straight ahead at the wall, Mr. Watson,"

I obliged.

"Do you live on Grantline Road?"

"Yes."

"What is your mother's name?" He paced his questions slowly and deliberately.

"I have two mothers. One is named Martha Velia and the other is Betty Price." I said that in one breath, not realizing where the words came from.

"Excuse me, Mr. Watson?"

"I was adopted. My adoptive mother is Martha. I've never met my birthmother..."

"Okay." He sighed. "I can see you are a little nervous. Forget about that question. Let me ask you, have you ever consumed any illegal drugs within the past six months?"

In the past six months? I was getting ready to spill my guts that I was busted for Panama Jack at fourteen.

"No, sir," I answered.

He paused, then made a few scratch marks on his notes. The polygraph machine continued to whir.

"Have you ever taken anything of value within the last six months?"

Then the postcard from Community Hospital somehow intruded into my mind! I suddenly wished there was a thumbtack in my shoe where I could pierce my toe and send the machine into a frenzy. "Yes!" I admitted. "I took a postcard from a hospital when I was nineteen years old."

"A postcard?" The polygrapher shrugged.

"Yes. It was where I was born..."

"Mr. Watson, I am speaking about *anything of value*. I don't mean candy bars or paper clips that you might have taken as a child. Now, let's start over. Have you ever stolen *anything of value* within the last six months?"

Wait a minute, I thought. I had just caught on to this *six months* thing. Then I realized that I could have safely kept those chairs that I had returned the day before.

"The only thing I have ever taken is two chairs from my college but I returned them yesterday."

"When did you take these chairs?"

"Two years ago." The silence was disturbing. I could feel my heart in my chest.

"Two years ago? And you returned them yesterday?" Was that a question, I wondered? He rolled his eyes and continued. "Other than the two chairs that you took from your college, have you ever taken anything of value within the last six months?"

"No," I answered solidly.

I continued to stare at the wall. The sound of the machine broke the silence.

"Okay, Mr. Michael. We're done."

"Do I get the job?" I asked.

"It is your employer's decision whether to hire you. We only give the data to them." He gave a half smile and ushered me out the door.

My palms were sweaty, one of the variables the polygraph machine measures. I was also positive that the darn gadget detected the throbbing of my heart. Anyway, I wiped the moisture on my pants and went home.

I departed downstairs to the small studio I had assembled to finish a recording mix of a song. Dad appeared around the corner as the final chord resounded.

"What do you think of that one?" I asked him while fading the volume slider.

"Crit, you know I don't understand all that racket. That's just a waste of time and money," he said, viewing the pulsating red lights from the console. I was never fond of my middle name, and my mind rummaged to find other words that started with 'cr': creep, crap, crud, crumb, and crotch. The rhyming words seemed equally disgusting. Spit, zit, sh... "You're just one in a million, Mi-kel. Don't you realize the percentage of people who fail at that silly racket?"

Very, very small, I thought humbly to myself. Dad was always street smart.

The next day the manager at Shalaars called. He told me to come to work the following Saturday at nine o'clock sharp. I got the job. I took a deep breath and told my parents. Mom was delighted. Dad's only concern was how much it paid.

I arrived promptly in my blue suit and clamp-on tie. My first duty was sweeping the floor. And this was a *glamorous* job, I jested to myself. Besides being dressed more formal, the only difference in sweeping the floors at Shalaars was that I would be using a vacuum cleaner instead of a broom.

Someone had rested a styrofoam cup full of hot coffee on the edge of the sales counter. After making about six or seven revolutions with the vacuum, I somehow wrapped the electrical cord around the cup, and launched it into the air on the manager's light brown suit.

He said an expletive. Then he repeated it three more times. Pointing his finger at the table edge he snarled, "I don't want anyone to ever set their coffee cup here again!" I imagined the cursed table turning into smoke and disappearing into oblivion. At least I was off the hook and was careful with the final strokes of the sweeper.

So inaugurated the new epoch of my life. I would sell rocks by day and strum rock by night. The main difference was that the diamond business would pay me a salary.

Coming home, I would unlatch the metal clamp of my tie and toss it across my shoulder. The TV would be on. An irritating announcer on Channel 3 would always blare the bad news of the day. Dad would be watching from his ring-side seat as he cautiously poked Mom's dinner into his mouth. I would hunt for leftovers, sometimes finding a delicious cold leg of fried chicken on the stove. Then I would dive down the steps into my private world.

10. *Mountain To Heaven*

Special Reading

Tommy Higgins's family moved southwest to Hopkinsville, Kentucky. Summer changed quickly into Autumn or *Indian Summer* as the residents called it. I drove down the next day and stayed overnight. The next morning Tommy took his cousin Steve and me to Pilot Rock, a mountain site that was renowned in his new homeland.

Arriving early, we jumped out of the car and raced to the top. Primitive stepping stones were awkwardly arranged in threes with an offsetting platform that made us look like galloping ostriches. Suddenly the bright sun disappeared as we spiraled up the huge cliff, for the steps led us to the mountain's center before it carried us upward.

An escalator would have been much more comfortable and there would be less chance of me scraping my clothes on a muddy rock. I was never much of an outdoorsman and never enjoyed mosquitoes, sharp thorny plants, and large bees that buzzed at low-frequencies. Tommy and Steve didn't complain so I stayed close behind them.

Embraced by a bright yellow light, we knew we were at the summit. An endless ocean of multi-colored Autumn trees blanketed the earth warmly. For the first time I grasped the magnificent size of the world. Although a complete circle revealed endless miles, I knew the view was such a small fraction of our mother planet. The air was chilly, I had forgotten to bring my coat, and there was unbelievable silence.

A huge fire tower was at the mountain's top. It was seven stories tall with twenty steps dividing each floor. Before we started to climb, however, we noticed that the fourth set of stairs was missing. Nevertheless, we climbed, praying that there wasn't another such occurrence at a higher level.

When we reached that fourth level we used the wooden beam above us to catapult our bodies across the missing steps. With fearless hearts and careful footing, we escalated into the sky. The air blew cooler on my arms and face. Fighting gravity, we dared not look down until we reached the highest point of the tower. Viewing the earth from this elevation was a spiritual awakening -- a complete freeing of one's soul. Tommy flapped his arms and pretended to fly. The glorious exhibition of Earth seized my breath. I could see a larger radius of multi-colored miles as I turned in a circle. I peered downwards. The trees were tiny but enormous in quantity.

Suddenly a chill ran through my heart. Although my confrontations with death had become familiar, I was overwhelmed with its recurring fear. I was miraculously rescued from the peril of winter near Featheringill Road. A strategically placed boulder had also given me extra Earth-Time just before the *Biscuit* was ready to plunge into the abyss of the Knobs. But surely some mischievous youngster or teenager that partied too much had come to Pilot Rock and did fall to his demise. I could not escape the dreadful feeling that a misplaced foot would trip me to the land of the non-living. Atop the tower, I clutched the side beams with white knuckles as I stared down.

I remembered movies where people fell from high places. The screams of the doomed were similar. I imagined losing my grip, slipping, then falling to the earth below. I envisioned grasping at air, for there was nothing to hold on to once detached from the tower. The free fall that would last a mere six or seven seconds would be more terrifying than one could imagine. The scrapbook of one's life would be played -- at lightning speed. Spectators would experience the solid proof to our mortality.

From out of nowhere the mystery of my birthmother haunted me, and that is why I wrote this chapter. The numbness of the breeze gave me an illusory high, and I became aware of my microscopic self. What if I was a victim of Pilot Rock, I imagined? If I died, then the secret of my creation would also die. The hope for a biological reunion would be concluded.

I glanced over to Tommy and Steve. The wind was peacefully blowing at their faces while they continued to absorb the panorama. They both wore pleasant smiles.

Leaning snugly against a tower brace, I tightly covered my ears with my hands and closed my eyes. I prevented any wind from seeping through my fingers so I could not hear anything.

Complete silence. I was deaf.

Darkness. I was blind.

This is death, I thought. After a moment I removed the burden from my senses and again gazed into infinity. The world was so big. I was so small.

In the evening I drove back to New Albany with a new but undefined awareness. For the first time since I was a toddler, I again realized the immensity of a power that is bigger than ourselves. Although we are all born from the wombs of the extraordinary creature we call woman, it is God who is our primal Mother. If I fell from the tower of Pilot Rock, my death would not upset the itinerary of the universe in the slightest, and it would be impossible for me to die without knowing my true creator.

11. *Mother's Day*

It was 1983, and Mom brought back a small pot of marigolds from Grantline United Methodist. I gave her a gigantic card that I had playfully scribbled twelve roses on with a bright red crayon. To Mom, it was my thought and efforts that were priceless to her. I don't remember her ever yearning for material things. She squeezed me with both arms before I descended downstairs.

I lifted my acoustic guitar from its stand and dragged my fingers across the strings. Mother's Day was always a joyous occasion for me and Mom, but at the same time it would submerge me into deep introspection. Maybe Mother's Day should be doubly joyous, I thought, for I had two Moms! One who raised me from birth and the other one whom I haven't met...yet.

Mom and Dad had told me about Dr. Turner and Raymond Grimes. They were the key characters of my adoption. Mom had said that Grimes was a "very old man" when I was born. I was now twenty-five so he certainly had aged the same number of years. He was either unthinkably old or dead. I assumed the latter.

Returning my instrument to its resting place, I phoned Indianapolis information for a listing of Turner M.D., William. I couldn't believe I had waited so long to take on such an effortless but obvious endeavor. The operator answered immediately and gave me the number, as if she were awaiting my call. I began to dial.

"Hello?" an older woman's voice answered.

"Hello, Mrs. Turner?"

"Yes?"

I realized I was listening to the voice of a woman whose husband delivered me. It was the closest connection I had ever made.

"My name is Michael Watson. Is Dr. Turner there?"

"Who is this?" she answered skeptically.

"My name is Michael Watson. Your husband delivered me in 1958. I was adopted then, and I am searching for my birthmother."

That last statement did not bring joy to the old lady, for she said that her husband died several years ago.

"I'm sorry to hear that. Are there any records left?" I grasped, not taking a breath in between sentences. "Is there any information about my birthmother?"

"There are no more records. I'm very sorry," she responded humbly.

"But what about the hospital. Don't they have records?" I asked involuntarily, already knowing that answer.

"I'm sorry. There are no more records, but good luck to you." Then she hung up before I thought of another question.

Later that day I surfaced upstairs to tell Mom about that phone call. She looked at me with the familiar face that was a cross between wonder and disappointment. "Michael," she paused, "are you still looking for your birthmother?"

"Sure, Mom. You know I love you, but sometimes I have a little empty feeling."

"What would you ever do if you found her? Would you want to go live with her?"

"Of course not," I said emphatically. "I want to know who she is, that's all. I have the right to know where I came from. I want to know..." I searched for words, "what is my nationality."

"Michael, what if you find her? What are you going to do then? Maybe she has had a hard life. And what if she would want you to take care of her? Maybe she doesn't have much money and would want you to support her." She continued to ramble. "Michael, I lived in fear for several years thinking that one of these days your birthmother would find you and ask for you back. You can't *realize* what I felt." She started to cry.

"What do you mean, Mom?"

"Michael, don't you understand that a social worker could have taken you away from us? Every time I heard a knock on the front door I thought it was either your birthmother or a social worker."

"Mom, please!" Then I wished I kept my mouth shut in the first place. We had had this dialogue many times before. I realized that I could never have the same feelings as an adoptive parent. But on the other hand, I don't think my Mom could ever comprehend my feelings. In fact, sometimes it was hard for *me* to define why I hungered relentlessly to search for the unknown.

"Michael, just remember that *I* am your mother." Her tears receded, and she spoke with a solid boldness I had never heard before. "I don't want you to ever forget that. Do you understand?"

I could never bear to see Mom cry, but that was a moment I could not manage to give her an assuring hug. I came to the appalling realization that this whole adoption game had become a tournament between me and Mom.

We can appreciate the beauty of a sunrise only when we have waited in the dark.-- Author unknown.

12. *Behind The Curtain Of Fear*

I have many fond memories of Shalaars. Sheila Carr would toss Planters cheese balls into my mouth from across the room while the manager was out. Roger would stalk the front door for an approaching jewelry prospect, extinguishing his cigarette into the ashtray as soon as the door opened, and making a quick swish through the air to dissolve the floating smoke. Margaret Clemmons once striped a customer's credit card into the manual imprinter and somehow caught her breast in it. And I accidentally caught my tie inside a jewelry showcase while bending over and locking the door. When I raised up, the tie locked me into a hunched position. Then it detached! Everyone was shocked in amazement. Then they laughed hysterically. Apparently they had never seen a clamp-on tie before. It looked like one of my limbs had been detached like the cartoon depictions of a leprosy victim.

Resuming an upright position, I confessed that I didn't know how to tie a tie. The next day I bought several regular ties and commenced the laborious learning process of knotting a double windsor. Even afterwards, the employees would secretly lift my collar just to make sure I wasn't wearing a phony. The consensus was that we did *not* sell imitation diamonds, the hanging plants were *not* artificial, and I should *not* wear fake ties.

Although I enjoyed working at Shalaars, slow periods would send me on a voyage of introspection. On many occasions I visualized Dad showing me his worn, wrinkled hands and saying, "You see these, Crit? They have worked hard all their life."

I was grateful to have such a job where I didn't have to exert so much physical labor and lift heavy pipes like him. Mom said that was the reason they sent me to college. Here I was, wearing a suit and a crisp white shirt, in which all I was lifting were polished diamonds. I sometimes felt guilty, knowing they had sacrificed much of their savings for my education.

During one playful moment, Sheila asked my nationality. I smiled and answered stupidly, "I don't know. I'm adopted." She then asked if I ever wondered who my birthmother was. My smile turned more serious and I answered affirmatively. I also told her all the sketchy information I knew about my human beginnings.

"Then go find her!" she said demandingly.

I couldn't manage to reach her level of inspiration. "I already made two trips to Indianapolis," I replied. "They said the books are sealed. It's the law."

I came home very somber. I knew I was denied a very fundamental human gift: my ancestry. I pulled out the family photo album from the living room desk and flipped its pages. The first photo showed Mom holding me on her lap. The unmistakable signs of a proud mother shone from her face. Another picture showed Dad wrestling with me on the couch. He wore a bright smile that I had never before recalled. Then came my birthday scenes: one year old, two years old, three years old. At five, I was smiling behind my birthday cake while Dad helped me hold up five fingers. On the next page I was blowing out six candles. The next showed seven plastic horses parading around another cake.

Then I returned to the first page. My hair was dark and curly. The eyes were dark and huge. I compared my photos to my parents on the same page. Mom was plump and fair skinned with a roundish face. Dad was slim and lanky with light hair. What happened before page one, I asked myself? Was I even *born*?

I surely didn't resemble my parents. I have never resembled anyone on this planet, I reminded myself again. I quickly deduced that my birthmother was presently forty-five years old. I also knew that was a young age for a woman and that she would certainly be alive. Then I remembered when my adoptive mother was the same age many years ago. She was very attractive. I imagined my birthmother was equally beautiful.

Sheila Carr had reignited the embers in my soul to search for the past. Tomorrow was Friday, and my work schedule read "off" for the next two days. I planned my third journey to the capital of Indiana. This time I didn't tell my parents about my intentions. Every time I mentioned my search it always caused pain and disappointment.

Friday was incredibly hot, and the Camaro didn't have air conditioning. I arrived at the city county building in the afternoon. Getting out of the car, I noticed my clothes sticking to my flesh from the suffocating humidity. The weather of Indianapolis seemed as unpredictable as New Albany: freezing one day and scalding the next.

This was my third trip to the probate court, which was the only institution I felt had any record of my early existence. While the familiar creaky elevator carried me upward, I wondered if Judge Jameson would recognize me and if he would give me a fat "no" before I even said hello. Would he even be there and would I have to start all over again with my interrogation? I mentally planned my request as I concentrated on the lighted floor numbers that slowly increased one by one. The other passengers stared at their feet.

"Your Honor," I began after entering his chamber, "My name is Michael Watson. I have made two previous trips to this court since I was barely old enough to drive a car. I was adopted on February 25, 1958 from Community Hospital by my adoptive parents who still reside in New Albany. Please, your honor, sometimes I don't know who or what I am. I have no history, no heritage, and no origin. Let me know who my birthmother was."

I stood straight, paced my words evenly, and kept constant eye contact. I then noticed that I wasn't interrogating but rather begging. As he looked at me with concrete eyes, an awful silence followed. The judge's appearance had not changed from the last eight years. I wondered if he recognized me, thinking "There is that darn kid again."

"Sit down, please," the familiar voice said. I obeyed. The judge gave me a long and penetrating stare, as if to ascertain my sincerity. He then intercommed his secretary. "Mrs. Green, please pull the court summary adoption records for Michael Watson, born two, twenty-five, fifty-eight. Make a copy and bring it to me."

The judge ruffled some papers on his desk without further eye contact as I sat quietly. Then a woman entered the room and handed the judge what appeared to be two pages stapled together. He took them and leaned way back into his mushy leather chair.

Devastating silence resounded once more. The judge remained expressionless as he scanned the document. The quietness was almost unbearable, and my mind created an artificial hum, like the sound of the wind on the tower of Pilot Rock. I was immediately consumed with a blend of aspiration and terror. The judge was holding the secrets of my personal universe in his hands. What was my nationality? Why did my mother relinquish me? Who *was* my birthmother?

Then he handed the papers to me.

"Here you are, Mr. Watson."

Fear embraced me with a tighter grip. Did I really have a right to see this information? I didn't know whether to look or not. Would I turn into a pillar of salt? Shouldn't I feel guilty for pursuing this? My adoptive parents are the only parents I've ever had. If it wasn't for them, I might not even be living on this earth.

I waited for the horror. I would now lift the veil imprisoning the dark forces of the past. The secrets of the unknown would finally be revealed as I drew the Curtain aside.

I reflexively took the papers and devoured the words faster than I could understand them. I feared that there was the possibility the judge could snatch the paper from my hands and say, "That's enough, Mr. Watson. You can come back again in ten more years."

But he didn't.

I relaxed, and reread the words from the beginning. It said:

Prepared by: Marion County Department of Welfare
Child Welfare Division
Mrs. Hazel Wilcox, Visitor
Court Docket No. 3-336
DPW Case No. E-38-02892

Date of Placement:	February 28, 1958
Date of Summary:	June 16, 1958

Name of Child:	Michael Crit Price
Date of Birth:	February 25, 1958
Status:	Illegitimate
Place of Birth:	Indianapolis, Indiana
No. of brothers or sisters:	1 half-brother
Property or inheritance:	None
Color:	White
With Whom Living:	The child is living with Stoy and Martha Watson, Grantline Road, New Albany, Indiana.
By Whom Placed:	The child was placed by the mother's physician (unnamed), the attorney, Raymond Grimes taking care of legal details, including an order from Probate Court to remove the baby from the hospital.

FATHER OF CHILD:

No information was secured about the father.

MOTHER OF CHILD:

Mrs. Betty Price was interviewed in the office, following arrangements made by her attorney, Raymond Grimes. She came from Plymouth, Indiana, her home and will return there, she said, by the next bus.

Mrs. Price was a small woman, wore her hair in a pig-tail. She said she knew nothing about the father of this baby. Some mutual friends had introduced them, and the child was conceived after they had too much to drink. She never saw her baby, and it was all like a bad dream.

She grew up with her parents (whose names she refused to give) and they were good people. When she was in the sophomore year, she quit school to be married. She was only 16 years old. She married Floyd Price, December 29, 1951. He was 26 years old. A child was born to them in 1953, named Michael David Price. On September 15, 1955, she divorced Mr. Price. She said he was never true to her.

She wanted nothing to happen to her first child, and that is why she would give us no more information about him or her family. She did say her parents lived near Noblesville, Indiana.

It was felt that Mrs. Price was not telling the truth and that she had been told what to tell our agency.

SIBLINGS:

There is one half sibling, Michael David Price. Nothing is known about him, except he is living with his maternal grandparents.

I suddenly wished someone was there with me. My energy drained. I didn't understand the unfamiliar words, people and places.

"What does this mean?" I asked the judge brainlessly.

"Well, for one thing, it looks like you have a half-brother... Michael David."

"You mean that wasn't me?"

"No, you are this person," pointing to Michael Crit Price.

"I have a brother?" I repeated.

"Yes, and his name happens to be Michael also. He would be...five years older than you."

"What should I do now?" The judge seemed to take on the mythical configuration of the birthfather I never knew.

"Well, it says here your mother's parents lived near Noblesville. Noblesville is just a few miles up the road past Carmel. Her parents could still be living there. Your mother never gave her maiden name. You might go to the courthouse there and see if you can find a copy of her marriage license to this Floyd Price. Then you will be able to find out who your grandparents are."

His words were like magic. When I shook hands with the judge, my energy level multiplied to that of Hercules. I returned to my car in which the interior was now blistering hot. I rolled down the windows and tried to keep cool from the onrushing wind as I sped to Noblesville.

I became oblivious to everything surrounding me. My eyes hardly veered off the long road even as I passed the slower moving automobiles. After passing the town of Carmel, I darted into the Noblesville exit, instinctively finding the old courthouse and raced inside.

"Hello," I said, directing my words at the first person I saw. "Can you please find me the records of Betty Pri... uh, Betty *Somebody* who married a Floyd Price around..." I searched the court summary, "... December 29, 1951?"

"Mister, we are closing now," came a woman's voice from my right. *Closing*? I looked at my watch. It was two minutes before four in the afternoon. Another lady saw my urgency and started to dig into the files.

"Please hurry, Ma'am," I said involuntarily.

"I'm going just as fast as I can, Sir."

The other employees watched me in confusion.

"I found my mother," I announced to everyone with radiance. "I was adopted. I have never known my birthmother until now. I'm going to find her today."

Two elderly ladies behind the counter smiled at each other. "How wonderful." I heard one say. "He was adopted. Isn't that precious?"

The lady who was digging returned. "I'm sorry sir. There's no information here. All I need are the names. Can you repeat those one more time?"

"Floyd Price is the man. I don't know Betty's maiden name."

"That's exactly what I checked, sir. There's no such..."

"Check some more!" I blurted. "I mean, there must be some record in there," my voice dropped to a more professional level.

The lady returned to the files hesitantly and shuffled again.

I yelled across the counter. "I have the date. December twenty...."

"We don't need the date," she interrupted. "I checked every Price that was married in Hamilton county. There is no one that matches that name."

The ladies' smiles faded into expressions of concern. The file lady turned to them and shook her head apologetically.

I started to feel sick. I wearily glanced at the court summary, then handed it to the lady. They all joined together in reviewing the people and places and told me there was nothing more they could do.

I stepped outside into the windless humidity and inspected the surroundings. Noble Nowhere-ville, I mused sarcastically. Then I began a brisk walk and increased my gait with every step.

My underarms and insides of my thighs were soaked from perspiration. I needed fresh clothes. There was a laundromat down the street and I aimlessly headed in that direction before I realized that I would have to sit naked while waiting for my clothes to wash and dry. I went to a drug store two doors down and purchased some deodorant, a toothbrush and small tube of toothpaste. Then I walked across the street to a discount clothing store and purchased a new pair of pants and a shirt. I changed in my car in front of the courthouse. The hot seat scalded my legs.

I studied the court summary more carefully. 'It was felt that Mrs. Price was not telling the truth...' The words haunted me. But the facts were so specific! If a twenty-two year old woman would lie, then she wouldn't have given such detailed information. She refused to give her parents' names. That was alright. It would make my search a little more interesting. I continued reading.

'When she was in her sophomore year, she quit school to be married.' She obviously went to Noblesville High School. I walked around the corner to the town library in my new bright red sleeveless shirt and stiff blue jeans...shorts weren't hip. I blindly riffled through the high school yearbooks from 1952, the year she would have been a sophomore. I didn't know her last name so I just looked for every Betty, Betricia, etc. I could find. There were none. Then I found myself scanning for my own reflection. Most everyone seemed very average and American-looking. The young boys had their hair slicked back strangely and the girls had weird hairdos.

As I flipped the pages, I remembered that I did not even allow my own junior picture to be published in the yearbook. What if she had the same low self-image as I did during those years of tribulation that every adolescent suffers? Should I have been looking for a, 'Sorry, No Photo?' I then looked in the years preceding and succeeding. No luck. The court summary was becoming damp from my sweaty hands so I made a copy before the former one disintegrated.

With my elbows on the desk, I relaxed my chin in the cup of my folded hands as the sun turned red and poured a horizontal beam of light above my desk. The library was closing in forty-five minutes. Then I thought: 'She married Floyd Price, December 29, 1951.' Maybe there was an announcement in the local newspaper. If I found that, then it would also give her parents' names. The reference clerk handed me a microfilm of the Noblesville Topics newspaper for two weeks up until the date of my birthmother's marriage. I scanned the film unsuccessfully until the library closed.

Most of the local businesses had shut down for the evening, and the residents seemed to evacuate back to their homes. I roamed the town by foot until the sky got dark and paused by a nearby phone booth. Since I still lived at home, I knew Mom would be deliriously worried by now.

"Hi, Mom."

"My God, Michael, where are you?"

"In Noblesville. It's about fifteen miles north of Indianapolis. Mom, guess what?"

"What?"

"I have a brother!"

"Michael, I know you like to kid your poor old mom. Where are you?"

"I went to Indianapolis again. The judge gave me a copy of the court summary of my adoption. I'm getting close to finding my birthmother. I'll be home tomorrow. Don't worry about me. I love you."

"Michael! Don't hang up! Wha..."

"Mom, my brother's name is *Michael,* the same as mine! I love you more than anything, Mom, but this is something I need to do. I hope you understand."

"MICHAE..."

"Good-bye." And I hung up.

Digging through my pockets, I could only exhume a few dollars and some change. I looked for a cheap place to sleep and ended up at the White Horse Inn. The room was small, the floors were buckled, and there was no phone. The bed was framed with ancient wrought iron and fashioned jagged curls in the headboard. The sheets were folded down white and crisp. I lifted the pillow and buried my face into it. It smelled fresh.

I removed my clothes and twisted the single faucet knob on the shower. The water was ice cold. The owners of the White Horse were obviously frugal with their utility expenses. The coldness momentarily revived my senses but did not facilitate my exhaustion. Nevertheless, I felt clean. I crawled into the bed, and the weight of my body sank into the abyss of the soft mattress. I felt my bones melt. The bed and I became one.

I looked up at the ceiling. Then down to the floor. To my left. Then to my right.

No spiders. I clicked off the light.

I awoke to a thin, bright stream of Saturday sunshine that found its way from the small opening of the curtains into my eyes. I was on a secret mission, a crusade to find the mystery woman. And now also my brother! I checked out early to explore the town.

I leaped into the Camaro, now rusting from the salt that is splayed onto Indiana's winter roads, and rolled the windows down. The morning air was cool and damp. So this is where my birthmother was from, I thought as I meandered through the streets. Maybe this is where I was conceived, where the egg and sperm united to create this body in which I now dwell. Maybe it was a one-night stand at the White Horse Inn. I managed a suppressed chuckle.

I came to a small church, parked my car, and entered. I heard singing from a distant room. Although I didn't see anyone, it sounded like the voices of six or seven adults trying to learn a hymn for the first time. I tiptoed my way to what looked like a tiny office. I found what I was looking for: a telephone and a fresh directory of Noblesville and surrounding towns.

Sitting at the small desk I discovered only about twenty Prices listed. The phone was a rotary style and evoked memories of the old phone in the elderly folks' house in Indianapolis. I glanced around the room and saw a handsome depiction of Jesus on a wall. I closed my eyes, trying to drown out the off notes from the choir. Before I began the first number, I had my finger in the phone hole with the letter "M". Then for good luck I continued to dial "O" and then "M" again to spell the code word of my mission. I also realized that I had just dialed "666," and my aspirations slightly dwindled. Nevertheless, I inhaled deeply and proceeded with the process of elimination.

"Hello, my name is Michael Watson," I commenced to the first number. "I am adopted. The reason I am calling is because I am searching for my birthmother. Her name became Betty Price after she married Floyd Price. I also have a half-brother named Michael David Price. Do *any* of those names sound familiar to you?"

Although my script got better with each call, every person that answered gave me a negative response. My leads were finished.

I solemnly drove to Noblesville High School. I parked in front, turned off my motor, and mostly just stared into the empty windows. I felt cosmically connected to the small town. Many thoughts traveled through my mind as I gazed. 'She quit school at 16... was a sophomore.' Why did she quit school so early? She didn't get pregnant with Michael David until three years later. Then I thought, I was not the first born. Why did she decide to keep Michael David but put me up for adoption?

I drove around haphazardly for the rest of the day. A few pedestrians scampered around here and there. I realized that this excursion had come to an end. Sunday was a busy day at Shalaars. I had to get back home.

Although the courthouse was closed, I tacked a copy of the court summary on the front door with my name and phone number at the bottom. I had also taken a black marker and inked through, "the child was conceived after they had too much to drink." Nobody's business.

I pulled into our driveway around seven in the evening. Peeking through the living room curtains was Mom's silhouette. I opened the familiar wooden door.

"Hello, everyone!" I greeted.

"So, you went back to Indianapolis. Well, what did you find out?" Mom asked with worry and anticipation. Dad lowered his newspaper just below his eyes to hear my answer.

"Here you are." I handed the court summary to them.

"What's this?" Mom asked.

"The judge gave it to me, Mom. This is the story of my life."

"How did you get this? I thought they said the records were sealed." Mom said.

"Never take 'no' for an answer, Mom."

We took turns reading the summary.

"So Price was her *married* name," Mom continued.

"Looks like you got a half-brother, Crit." Dad smiled. I was proud to share this new information with my parents, and that I was tenacious enough to get it. Then I heard Dad keep repeating, "PLYmouth, PLYmouth Indiana," accenting the first syllable strongly.

We reread the summary together: "She came from Plymouth, Indiana, her home and will return there, she said, by the next bus." After locating a map, we saw the city was almost at the northern tip of the state. "That's right, Dad," I said. "But her parents were from Noblesville. I would be on a wild goose chase if I went to Plymouth, not knowing her maiden name."

Then before we retired for bed Mom said, "Me and your daddy are really happy for you, Michael. Don't you feel better knowing that your search is finally over?"

"What do you mean, Mom?" I asked.

"Well, you got the information you wanted, didn't you? You know where you birthmother came from and the circumstances. When she gave birth to you she had been divorced from Floyd Price. Back then people didn't have very much money. She probably couldn't afford to keep you."

"But Mom, I haven't found her yet," I argued. "I just want to meet her at least one time. Don't you understand?"

"Michael, didn't you read what it said at the bottom?" Her finger went precisely to the beginning of the sentence. "It says right here that she probably lied about the whole thing. You could be searching for the rest of your life for nothing. You could be spending money on top of money. Then if you did find her she could be an alcoholic, with no money, and then you would feel obligated to support her."

"Mom, for Pete's sake!"

"I'm just telling you the truth. I don't want you to be hurt. You should thank God that you have parents who love you very much. Do you realize that we couldn't love you any more than your other friends' parents?"

The pride of my two-day achievement gradually resolved into shame. I didn't know *what* I felt anymore.

"And I hope you don't think about driving clear to Plymouth," she continued. "We worried enough about you for the past two days."

"But Mom..."

"Michael, if and when you find your birthmother, I am behind you all the way. Just don't ever forget that me and your daddy are your *real* parents. What if your birthmother couldn't afford to put braces on your feet when you were a baby? You would be walking like the poor old man I saw at the store today. You should have seen him, Michael, the poor guy. One foot went straight out to the left, and the other went straight out to the right."

This time Mom did not get upset or cry. Her words were straightforward and had a sense of finality.

"PLYmouth. PLYmouth." Dad read the summary over and over until late in the night.

13. *Where Is Michael Watson's Family?*

I strolled into work proudly the next day. "Well, guys, my birthmother was short, beautiful, and wore her hair in a pigtail!," I beamed.

"You found her?" Sheila Carr cheered.

"Not exactly. But ..."

My two-day adventure was the talk of the day. The employees and manager took turns reading the court summary. They bombarded me with questions like, "Now why don't you try this?"..."Why don't you try that?"...and "Did you try...?" My answers were always the same, "Yes. I tried that, did that, done that. Thank you."

I was very fortunate, I thought, to possess the sacred information that had been so secretly protected since my birth. Maybe it was a lesson that confirmed one can really obtain anything in this world with genuine effort. It took all my will to eliminate the events of my journey from my thoughts while I waited on jewelry clients.

Later in the day I began to feel the same familiar hollowness in my soul. I wasn't satisfied with the court summary, for I still had the desperate need to see and know my birthmother. I became nauseated with the fear that this could really be the end of the saga. The last sentence echoed eerily in my mind --"It was felt that Mrs. Price was not telling the truth."

The phone rang and Margaret Clemmons handed the receiver to me, saying it was someone from Noblesville.

"Hello," I answered.

"Hello, Michael Watson?," said a middle-aged male voice.

"Yes."

"Mike, my name is Ernie Sullivan from the Noblesville Daily Topics newspaper. We were given a copy of a document that was pinned on the courthouse door." He spoke with a smile.

"Yes, sir, that was me."

"Mike, we were told by the ladies in the courthouse you were searching for your birthmother, whom you feel might have lived here in Noblesville. Actually, I believe you left a copy all over town, didn't you?" he chuckled.

"Yeah, I guess I did."

"We would like to do a story about your search, and maybe if there is anyone here that knows about your mother, they can contact you."

"That would be great!" My spirit immediately awakened. I proceeded to tell the reporter my life's story. On company time.

I hung up the telephone with renewed aspiration. The Shalaar's gang was waiting for my reply. I told them that I was going to be in the Noblesville newspaper.

The missing piece of my identity would soon be inserted into the puzzle of the past. Front page. Someone would call me from the coverage, I was sure. Maybe my birthmother herself. The reporter said the article would be in Wednesday's paper and that he would send me a copy.

No one called on Wednesday. On Thursday I got a manilla envelope addressed to me at Shalaars from the Noblesville newspaper. I opened it quickly and the front page blazoned in bold typeface: "**Where Is Michael Watson's Family**?"

The entire information was there (minus the connotation of Betty's drinking happenstance). It detailed the marriage, divorce, and gave the exact data from the court summary. Toward the bottom read, "In a telephone interview, Mike said he would like to hear from anyone who can provide information regarding his mother, father, half brother, or their families." It also gave my home address and the telephone number to the newspaper.

I waited patiently for the next week. I called my parents from work every day around eleven o'clock to ask them if I received any mail or if anybody called. Then the news was published again the following Wednesday, "**The Search Continues - No Success Yet.**" The employees encouraged me and said that someone was bound to contact me just from the publicity: Somebody will know somebody that knows somebody. Three weeks passed. Then four.

But nobody called. Nobody.

Another month passed. The excitement of the preceding weeks had settled and life resumed its normal state at the Watson household. I knew that the words printed on the court summary were like tiny keys that could unlock the secrets of the past. That document remained in a dark and top secret file, hidden from anyone's eyes for a quarter of a century. I knew this had become a very personal journey for me. Everyone enjoyed my story, but no one shared my obsession.

I browsed through my worn ALMA Search Book. I imagined my birthmother being as close as a local telephone call. She had now metamorphosed into a *real* person. Before my third trip to Indianapolis she was intangible. She was a mythical being, having no shape or substance. Interestingly, as a child I could easily create a mental picture of the *boogie man*. It was a monster that dwelled in the closets of little children. It had black fur, fang-like teeth, and red slits for eyes that would glow in the dark. My birthmother, on the other hand, was forever an apparition in my dreams. From the court summary, Betty Price had finally taken on a physical form, "...a small woman, wore her hair in a pig-tail."

I went to the bathroom mirror and peered so close that the glass fogged from my breath. Touching my face, I envisioned my features softened, with a dark brown pony tail. My birthmother's eyes were very dark like mine, I portended, but with the underlying expression of sorrow. I imagined her walking down the gusty streets of Indianapolis with her head down. As her hair would trail behind her, she would wonder about the child she never saw: the Relinquished One who would now be another's Chosen One. She would justify that the forsaking of her son was done in the name of love. She would have her words prepared if I ever knocked on her shabby door, "I wanted to keep you so much, my son, but because of my divorce and not having enough money to support even myself, I had no choice but to give you away. Please don't hate me."

I removed my hands from my face and returned to the ALMA Search Book. A paragraph mentioned how to obtain birth certificates and said that they include the *maiden* name of the mother. I figured I could obtain this if I pretended to be my half-brother. Then I would be able to find my grandparents, her closest relatives. I went to work on my old typewriter.

```
March 7, 1983

Indiana State Department of Health
Vital Records Division
1330 West Michigan Street
Indianapolis, IN 46206

To whom it may concern:

Please send me a copy of my birth
certificate. Enclosed is a money order
for the correct amount.

   Mother's name:   Betty Price
   Father's name:   Floyd Price
   Born:            1953
   Place:           Marion County

   Sincerely, Michael David Price
```

I realized how ignorant I was as I typed, and thought I would be laughed at for omitting the month and day Michael David Price was born. The court summary said she was from Plymouth. Although that statement could have been a false, I nevertheless increased my chances by typing variations of the letter, including Marshall and Hamilton counties.

I mailed them and waited. During the next few days I received reply letters that responded virtually the same: 'In order to obtain a birth certificate, it is necessary to include your mother's maiden name. We are returning your money order. Thank you.'

Memories returned of rejection letters from record companies. If one's song wasn't receiving air play on a radio station, a major record company would not be interested. The reverse was if a song had not already been picked up by a major record company, radio stations would not be interested.

I angrily ripped the last reply in half and crumbled it into the trash. Then I thought of every contradiction I had learned in life thus far, such as one cannot get a job unless they have experience for that job, or one cannot obtain credit unless they already have credit.

Several months later I repeated my request for a birth certificate using my own name and birth date. It was possible, I heard, that a negligent clerk could mistakenly pull the unamended copy and send it to me. I received my very official-looking *amended* birth certificate shortly thereafter from the Vital Records Division, pretending to convey that my biological parents were Martha Watson and Stoy Watson.

Sometime later I called Noblesville High School to find out who was the principal. I sent him a letter along with a copy of the court summary, saying I was hunting for my birthmother in his city. I politely asked him to scan the school's yearbooks and to see if there was a young girl named Betty that matched the description from the summary. Then I re-sent my letter a week later. I never did receive a reply from anyone at Noblesville High School.

Drearily, I ran out of clues. In 1984 I wrote the Marion County Department of Public Welfare.

ATTN: Manager
Child Welfare Division
Indianapolis, IN

I am an adoptee searching for my birthmother. Mrs. Hazel Wilcox was the

> caseworker involved in the proceedings. This is my second request in asking who has access to her records and whereabouts. I have a copy of the original court summary. I must have additional information in order to find her. Please respond.

And my answered letter:

> Due to the gigantic storage problem of closed records, the older ones have been destroyed. The information in our files regarding the study our agency made for the Marion County Probate Court is one of those expunged.
>
> Your placement was a non-agency adoptive placement which means that only one contact, the office interview, was had with your biological mother. The totality of information, which our caseworker obtained, would have been included in this report.
>
> Mrs. Hazel Wilcox retired over sixteen years ago. If she produced the same amount of studies as our present caseworkers, she would have completed more than 200 per year. There is no way that anything could be added to the data in the report she made to the court on June 16, 1958.

Although someone had once told me that there is a great joy when a social worker places a child, I also wondered if they fail to realize that adoptees eventually grow up and desire to know something as primal as who gave birth to them.

I remembered how the Noblesville Daily Topics caused such a front page commotion about my trip to their little town. I then became amazed, thinking about the consequences of being in the *Indianapolis Star*. Millions of people would read it, and it would be quite impossible to not find someone who knew about my beginnings. I dialed a reporter and did my best to get her excited about writing an article. She responded apologetically that adoptees looking for their birthparents are not really in the public's interest at the time, but that I could place an ad in the classifieds. I stifled a laugh before hanging up, imagining the headline, "Boy Looking For Mother. If you gave birth to me, please call."

14. *In Search Of California*

I gradually became a top salesperson for Shalaars. I came to work, gave my finest presentations, wrote up the sales tickets, and returned home. I would then disappear downstairs and work like a mad scientist in my music studio. I channeled every ounce of my bewilderment and energy into creative expression.

In 1985 I married a young girl named Ellen. We had been dating for the previous eight months. Coincidentally, two weeks later I was asked to manage one of Shalaar's divisions in Overland Park, Kansas. Ellen and I would fly there shortly afterwards for an orientation of my new position.

Overland Park was over five hundred miles from New Albany. It was a clean, modernized, but very strictly-governed town twenty miles from Kansas City, Missouri. Until then, I had never ventured very far from home. I realized that any ensuing attempts in my search would be stifled from the further distance. I would be pushed farther from my blood roots. Nevertheless, it was time to become completely self-sufficient, for I had just recently been weaned from the nourishment of my parents' refrigerator. I now had a companion to begin a new life in a new world.

My supervisor-to-be and his wife met us at the Country Club Plaza in Kansas City. His name was Hank Scarly and was a short, fast talker who seemed to avoid direct eye contact. Scarly flagged down one of the black horse and buggies that rode tourists through the plaza. Scarly and his wife enjoyed the view from the front seat. Ellen and I crouched in the back. As Scarly mumbled passing points of interest, my new bride and I were content with just absorbing the almost magical surroundings. We went to a restaurant afterwards.

"So what do you think about Kansas, Michael?" the supervisor asked after his last bite of filet mignon.

"I love it!" I exclaimed.

"Do you and your wife think you would enjoy working out here?"

"Oh, yeah. It would be really great, " I said.

"So what do you say about starting next week and we'll start you off at $...?"

So there it was. The infamous sales close. Spoken at that strategic moment after I shoveled a large spoonful of mint ice cream into my mouth. The initial salary was lower than I expected. The pressure was on. I swallowed hard. "I'm very sorry, Mr. Scarly. I don't think I will be able to come out here and work for so little money."

Scarly's eyes became unexpectedly larger from surprise. He fumbled with his spoon and asked harriedly, "Michael, what do you mean? We are offering you much more than you're currently making in Louisville? Plus think about all the bonuses and commissions you'll make as a store manager."

"That's true, but I've studied the cost of living out here." I spoke confidently, even though I had conducted no such research. "Living expenses are higher here than in Kentucky and Indiana. Utilities are higher because of severe winters and hot summers. Plus the state of Kansas has higher taxes on income and automobiles. I would have to receive at least one hundred and fifty dollars more per week before I could consider your offer."

The supervisor remained silent. I continued stuffing ice cream. His thoughts were as transparent as cellophane. Here he was, getting ready to hand his credit card to the waiter for an astronomical amount. He would also have to pay our night at the hotel. And lastly, the expense of air travel would be in vain.

"Let's go into the corridor and talk, Michael," he said with a forced smile.

Though unfinished with my dessert, I followed him where we could talk without our wives listening. From a distance, observers would be able to see our arm and hand gestures, signifying an unsuccessful conference.

Ellen and I returned to Indiana, then received a phone call from the vice president two days later upping the anny of my beginning wages by seventy-five dollars per week. We agreed to the higher earnings and flew back to Overland Park, where I lived for the next five years.

I had long accepted the uniqueness of being adopted and the intermittent curiosity of my roots had become a way of life. I would sometimes express feelings of voidness to my wife and the employees. I would wonder if my biological parents were in the jewelry business or were musically inclined. I wished I could thank them for the talents that they genetically bestowed to me. My eternal quest slowly disappeared, however, after I assumed the two simultaneous new titles of husband and jewelry store manager.

Less than a year later, Ellen unexpectedly called late at night to say she wasn't coming home. I rose from my pillow with a lackadaisical chuckle and asked if she was seeing someone else. She whimpered a "no." Noting her seriousness, I asked if she still loved me. She said she didn't know. I felt my bed quiver from my sudden fright and asked if she still wanted to be married. She replied the same, then said she would come to get her things while I was at work the next day.

There was no familiar chattering of the television as I entered our apartment the following evening, and the rooms had grown in size from the removed furnishings. She had not even left a telephone number, and I never heard from her again.

I prayed selfishly if she would return. My ignorance of not knowing my destiny was more agonizing than being prepared for a life of solitude and loneliness in a city that was light years from the place I was raised and christened *home*.

I wept. And then, from out of nowhere, I felt a serenity that completely penetrated my being. Although there was no actual voice or touch to my shoulder, there was a real presence that swept a gentle wave of peace through me. My anguish miraculously disintegrated, and I was assured that there was nothing in this world to *ever* be worried about. Latent memories of 1 Corinthians Thirteen comforted me in knowing better plans were in store for both of us.

We divorced a few months later. I attended a support group for those who had similar fates. It was an assembly of about twenty people, mostly women, who came to re-establish meaning in their lives. Most were victims of emotional abuse or infidelity, and one woman had been married for over twenty years.

It was extremely difficult to erase the thoughts of my short-termed wife. An underlying rage laid dormant in my soul for several months afterwards from jangling preconceptions of eternal marital bliss. I utilized my anger by becoming the paramount salesperson from the forty-store jewelry chain, acquiring several awards along the way.

The store surpassed its sales projections for the previous ten months and my income soared. The plump commissions allowed me to purchase my first house, conveniently one mile from the store, and complete with mature trees and a den for my music equipment. Shortly afterwards, as a final touch to the decoration of the driveway, I bought a beautiful red sports car.

The next thing I remember is Hank Scarly escorting me outside the store for a serious discussion. He admitted that although my personal sales never once faltered, my divorce seemed to estrange me from the rest of the employees, saying many complained that I refused paying attention to them when they spoke to me. The store's morale did seem to submarine, I remembered, but I never once thought I was a direct result of the lack of team spirit.

Induced by Scarly to take a tremendous pay cut, I transferred to an undesirable Shalaars across the state border in Missouri. It was in Krison's Square, a dilapidated shopping mall thirty-five miles away from my new home. My manager title was stripped away.

Living over five hundred miles from Indiana, I couldn't go crying back to Mom. The enigma became even more devastating than the divorce from Ellen, for I had been *married* to Shalaars for almost ten years. I was just starting to get over the tragedy of my short-lived marriage with the help of my friends at the support group, and now I was faced with another dilemma that would recreate a second divorce. Perhaps there was a deeper reason that Scarly demoted me to an entry-level salesperson. I resolved that I had acquired an artificial self-confidence as a defense mechanism from losing my wife. Even then, I felt it was ironic that I was ostracized from a store in which I generated most of the sales.

I had never completely quit smoking, and my multiple misfortunes seemed to intensify my urge for the disdainful habit. Then I developed a horrible cough that lingered for what seemed like an eternity. I had destroyed myself, I was sure. My father had always smoked, I remembered, and he never once restrained himself from the addiction. I could not blame heredity for the obsession, at least from my adoptive Dad. Like my father, I feared I had ruined my health on my on accord. Perhaps I had emphysema or worse!

While completing the lengthy applications in the doctor's office, I remembered my previous visits for the removal of my wisdom teeth and when I received stitches under my chin from falling alongside the pool in junior high. The blanks would always ask my nationality, race, and the medical history of my family. I also remembered my complete frustration and ignorance from not being able to answer a single question. Further down the form it would say, "In your family, are there any cases of: heart disease, epilepsy, tuberculosis, diabetes, high blood pressure?"

I would simply write "adopted" and ditto marks to the end of the form. I was overjoyed when the throat specialist diagnosed my malady as a common air virus. After prescribing some medicine, my cough finally subsided six weeks later. I had taped a makeshift calendar on my bathroom mirror, boldly X'ing every day with a black marker before I went to sleep, commending myself for not touching any tobacco. I resolved that if I could stop smoking for six weeks, I could stop forever.

And so I did.

Over the next few months, I reviewed my talents and decided where to best use them. I had no wife, no children, and no work place that I felt part of anymore. I was relatively free from obligations and could go anywhere I chose. On the other hand, I *did* have a mortgage, and monthly bills that unyieldingly filled my mailbox from utility companies, insurance collectors, and from the bank for my little red car. My debts soon overgrew my reduced salary.

Although a polished musician, I had never earned more than a few dollars from the craft, and the pessimistic words my father prophesied during my teenage years forever plagued me. I knew the possibility was slim that I would be able to make a living from music.

My other passion was selling jewelry. I felt worthy in helping a couple select a diamond ring that would symbolize their commitment to each other, a union which I privately hoped would last for a long time, or at least much longer than my marriage.

One evening at my kitchen table I unfolded a large map of the United States. I could go anywhere, I reasoned. I never liked remote areas, like our small farm in Indiana, and I always despised scraping ice from windshields and shoveling snow. I much rather enjoyed places with lots of people, action, and unlimited opportunities. I placed my fingers near Southern California. Although I had never been there, I imagined the palm trees and warm climate. While Los Angeles measured only nine ruler inches from Kansas City, the map legend equated each inch to one hundred fifty-six miles. I caught myself smiling, and somewhere between depression and anticipation I mentally created my destiny for the next world. Even though I was a store manager for the past five years, I realized that I never really had autonomy, for large companies have so many levels of bureaucracy. In California I could get a jewelry sales job, earn a good salary, and who knows, might eventually own a jewelry company.

Krison's Square drew patrons who would rather steal jewelry than buy it, and the police and security personnel would always be toting those caught in the act with handcuffs down the walkway. The days went by painfully slow, and I would try to awaken myself whenever my new manager would pass. Any asking price on jewelry beyond one hundred dollars would make customers think twice. During breaks I would scan the classifieds in the trade magazines: WANTED: Experienced Sales for west coast, NEEDED: Jewelry line salesman for California, etc.

After preparing fifty resumes I mailed them to the Golden State. The few prospective employers who replied said that there was no consideration for employment unless they first met the applicant. The jewelry business was based on trust, they explained, and it would be impossible to hire anyone from a mere written description or telephone conversation.

My funds continued to shrink and I relinquished many personal belongings. After much grief, I put my house and car up for sale. I told Scarly that I was going to get a less expensive auto and rent an apartment. I was not lying, but I failed to tell him I was planning on moving fourteen hundred miles away.

During lunch I would sneak to the public phone booth and retrieve a list of California jewelry vendors that I had stashed in my pocket. They all responded the same, and I finally realized the necessity of going there.

I purchased a dirty brown-colored Mustang that had twice the mileage of my red car and accepted the first offer on my house.

Although Mom and Dad didn't agree with everything I did, they were the people I loved the most. Whether they approved or not, I always wanted to tell them about my dreams. I quickly learned to despise rotary telephones, and it felt nice to dial that familiar number from my push buttons.

"Mom," I began, I'm moving to California. Don't worry about me."

"California? My Lord, Michael! Why are you going to California?" Mom was always the one who answered the phone, even though Dad would probably be sitting right next to it. "Answer the phone, Veeler!" I imagined him saying before Mom picked up.

"There's nothing left for me out here, Mom. I've given this much thought. I'll get a job there. I'll be fine."

"Michael...me and your daddy would *never* get a chance to see you anymore! California? Who do you know in California?"

"Nobody," I admitted.

"Michael, I know you don't like being told what to do. Lord knows you never want to listen to your mom. But...," she spoke without pause. I listened patiently for what I knew was coming next. "Have you thought about who in the world will help you move all your furniture? What are you going to do when you get out there? My word, Michael, work is hard to find. What if you can't get a job? Then what are you going to do?"

"Mom. I love you. You'll never have to worry about me. Remember how you taught me how all things are possible?" Then I remembered it was actually Mom who indirectly encouraged me to do the impossible: get a copy of my adoption court summary.

"Michael, please give this some more thought, honey," she implored, ignoring my question. "I know you are a good salesman and you're smart, but that doesn't mean that there are any jobs in California to be had. Oh, boy. Wait till your dad hears about this. We'll worry to death about you."

After a few minutes we hung up.

From longevity, I had accumulated a four-week vacation. Without wasting time, I set up several employment interviews. On the first day of my vacation, unbeknownst to Scarly or anyone at Shalaars, I flew to Los Angeles.

I sat alone on the plane, mostly just staring out the window. I scribbled notes in my binder, trying to make out an itinerary of my four-day stay. I suppose my actions were quite preposterous, and I really did not know a soul in the state of California. But just as ridiculously, I possessed a confidence that had surfaced from somewhere in my past. My life was unfolding on this very day, I had convinced myself. I dreamed about a tropical climate, new friends, and the challenge of braving a new world.

A nervous throb emerged in my throat as the plane touched the ground. At the baggage claim, I had never before seen such a mixture of nationalities. Hundreds of passengers, none which even remotely resembled myself, were gathered around the luggage tram waiting for the correct second to snatch the handles of their belongings.

I rented a car and searched for a place to sleep. The cash reserve in my pocket had dwindled. Since I wasn't afraid of shoddy hotels, I paid the first night's stay at one close by. The room that matched the number on my key reminded me of the White Horse Inn, except the ceilings were much taller and there was a phone by the bed. I wearily confirmed my appointments for the next day, took a familiar cold shower, and went to sleep. The next morning I dressed sharp and exited the hotel with many onlooking stares.

After a few interviews, it was inevitable that I would have to list a reference. I called my new manager at Krison's Square from a clamorous phone booth:

"Jason, this is Michael," I said loudly.

"Hello, Michael!" I always liked Jason Crandall. "Enjoying your vacation?"

"Jason, I need a reference," I said louder, plugging one ear tightly."

"I figured this would happen sooner or later, Michael. You know I can only say great things about you. Why is it so noisy?"

"I'm in downtown L.A."

"L.A.! And we thought you were looking for an apartment over here." And after a brief interchange, Jason said, "Michael, you have my warmest blessings, and I wish you the best of luck. Feel free to use my name anytime you wish."

"Thanks, Jason," I said. "You're great. Good-bye."

On my third appointment the interviewer said his company needed someone to work at one of their high volume stores forty-five miles south of Los Angeles. I drove there with a map I discovered in the back seat of my rental and braved the freeway swollen with thousands of cars. I exited from the 405 onto a much more peaceful street, then found my destination at Orange County's South Coast Plaza. It was an elegant jewelry store in a most beautiful part of Costa Mesa. There I negotiated a final salary and was asked to start in one week. I was later told that Jason Crandall had indeed delivered an outstanding reference, which beget the final decision to hire me.

I drove around the rest of the day and put a deposit on what was going to be my new home: apartment 902 at Driffly's Park. Then I flew back to Kansas to pack what was left of my possessions. I rented a huge bright yellow Ryder truck and connected my heavily-dented Mustang to the rear. Bidding farewell to my friends and neighbors, I began a three-day journey into an unknown galaxy.

America was so lonely. My radio did not work. My mind wandered infinitely. I thought about every event from my childhood until the present. I remembered Veronica Walsh, a salesperson I had hired in Overland Park. I always told Veronica that life was like a triangle, in which humans are always striving to reach a higher level than they are at presently. Her side was that life was like a circle, where we all eventually come to the same point from which we originated. Neither one of us could convincingly argue our viewpoints, but we always respected each other's opinions.

The mountains of Colorado dimly came into focus. As the truck sped nearer, the evening grew dark, and the mountains eventually disappeared into the blackness.

It wasn't until I was surrounded by the gigantic red rocks of Utah that I arose from what seemed to be true consciousness. The thought of the painful separation from Ellen writhed into my mind. I thundered affirmations over the raucous grunting of the engine that my marriage did not fail but was indeed a *success* for one year. I remembered when I cried for an answer, and I remembered the sensation of warmth on my shoulders I received as a divine reply.

Then I wept again. It seemed that the largest portion of my life had always been such a solitary quest, and I suddenly realized my aloneness. If Veronica Walsh's life-circle theory was correct, I would never be able to completely fulfill my life, for how could I return to the same point that I started if I never had an origin? As the thought of my birthmother crept into my mind, I again realized that I was denied a place on the X and Y axis of my human creation.

The compelling lure of the Pacific eventually aroused my senses again. I realized that I had nowhere in life to go but upward. I had no past, but I had the will to create my future. The large wheel in my grip transformed into the helm of my morrow. I could steer it left or steer it right. But for now I continued to travel linearly, with the sun at my back in the morning and blaring in my face in the evening. Grantline Road is where I was raised, I thought, but California would be my home.

On the third day I arrived in Santa Ana, a neighboring city of Costa Mesa, and plowed into the entrance of my new apartment complex with the old Mustang trailing behind the truck. It wasn't until that moment that I remembered Mom's frantic words, "Who's going to help you?"

Jumping to the ground, I gave my legs a good stretch and ambled to the management office for the key to my second-story apartment. The key said 902, but I knocked on door 903.

"Hi," I began, My name is Michael." A handsome, dark-skinned young man answered. "I'm going to be your new neighbor. If there's anything I can do for you, just let me know."

"¿Como?" was the reply. Unfortunately, my foreign language classes never included Spanish. Then four other young men appeared at the entrance. One who could speak better English than the others emerged in front.

"Hi. How are you?" he said.

"Great. Thank you. I was just telling your friend that I will be your new neighbor. If there is anything I can do for you or your friends, just let me know." I repeated my sales close word for word.

"Nice to meet you." Miguel welcomed a friendly hand. "If we do something for you, let us know too."

"Thank you. Do you and your friends like pizza and beer?" I spoke slowly as I gave exaggerated hand gestures. I was renowned for that anyway, and Dad said if I were born without arms I wouldn't be able to talk.

"Si. Yes," Miguel and two others nodded.

"If you can help me move a few of my things into my apartment, I will buy two large pizzas and some beer for all of us." I motioned again, maintaining a brisk smile although weary from the trip.

"Sure." Miguel looked towards the others for mutual consent. "We will help you."

"Great. Let's go!" My sales wrap up.

When the boys scurried around the corner, they seemed less enthusiastic when they saw the giant yellow truck that took up most of the parking lot. Nevertheless, Miguel clapped his hands as one does at the beginning of a laborious but necessary job, like mowing the lawn on a humid day. One by one, each boy grabbed a furniture leg and hauled it into apartment 902. They never once faltered in their pace. I worked equally hard.

Returning to the truck for my fifth armload I noticed an attractive, golden-skinned girl with long, almost black hair, walking hurriedly in the same direction as myself. Thinking I might not ever get another chance to talk to her I seized her attention.

"Hi, my name is Michael. I'm your new neighbor. If there's any..."

"Yeah. Okay. Thank you." She smiled pleasantly without listening. "I have to go. Bye." Then she left.

Her abruptness startled me, and her response was that of one who tries to get rid of a pesky door to door salesperson. I realized my greetings were becoming stale. I shrugged and continued towards the truck.

Forty-five minutes later the Latino gentlemen and myself all sat down to the now reassembled massive oak dining room table. I was hungry but too fatigued to eat. The young boys looked physically fit and unaffected from making so many trips up and down the steps. I was saturated with sweat. Fulfilling my promise, we consumed both pizzas and several beers.

Although the five gentlemen became good neighbors, I don't believe they volunteered any more favors.

My timing was right on schedule, and I went to work the next day. I awoke early to the California sun that brightened the walls of my new bedroom. My bones ached. I dressed in a fresh suit for the first time in a week and left for my new place of employment two miles away.

Before the day ended I sold a wedding band for several thousand dollars. Everyone including myself was amazed at my *beginner's* luck. South Coast Plaza was a new world in itself. The customers whom I remember balking at twenty dollar watch bands in Kentucky and Kansas were now buying one hundred and seventy-five dollar bands without flinching. This magnificent mall attracted a wealthy clientele that I had never seen before.

I enjoyed the glamorous surroundings, but I realized that my seniority as a ten-year jewelry veteran had been erased. Although hired at a generous salary, I despised the notion of playing the part of an entry-level jewelry employee, and I did not enjoy the dull process of learning foreign company policies.

As I returned to my apartment in the evening, I noticed the pretty girl from the day before. She was peeking out from the door below mine. Then, another woman's face appeared in the opening, motioning for me to come over. The woman introduced the mystery Guatemalan girl.

Her name was Maria del Carmen. This time she looked into my eyes. When she spoke, she delighted all of my senses. She was wondrously the first girl in California that interested me.

Other than a leftover slice of pepperoni and cheese, there was no food. I invited Carmen to the grocery store. Our first date. Excited as unattended children in a Toys R Us store, we filled the grocery cart past its rim without once looking at the individual prices. We talked so incessantly while driving back that we failed to see that the stoplights had changed to green. On three occasions the cars behind us beeped impatiently. Returning to the apartment, after helping me nail the final painting on the wall, Carmen introduced me to the delectable dining pleasure of fried banana, black beans, and corn tortillas.

I soon adapted to my new lifestyle, and I just as quickly began a love affair with the coastal breeze and mountains that I summoned from my apartment window. I lived every moment with the immense appreciation of being alive. Even though I cherished each day like a long-awaited vacation, I squeezed every ounce of pleasure from my days off by escaping to the beach. There the warm sand massaged my back and waves climbed just inches below my feet. The gentle roar of the ocean would perform stereophonically while the Pacific sun caressed my face and body.

With my new girlfriend and employer, the quest for my roots dissolved. I enjoyed the fast pace of Southern California. When highways were not jammed, automobiles seemed to travel at an average speed of twenty miles per hour over the posted limits. Even the speech and gait of the residents seemed faster than their midwestern counterparts. I would earn a living selling jewelry, come home and walk on the beach with Carmen with a blanket to shield ourselves from the cool ocean wind.

Carmen made me feel young and alive. English soon replaced her native Spanish dialect, and she became prolific in this second language much faster than I did hers. I remember the excitement of learning new words as we slowly mouthed the syllables. My goal of rehumanizing myself in a new world was being fulfilled, and the joy of being with Carmen healed every wound I suffered from the past.

15. *Gallery of Diamonds*

It was 1991. Jewelry sales had dwindled mercilessly during the past two years from a poor economy and during that time I had worked for many different employers without leaving the northwest corner of the mall. The first store implied rumors of a company takeover and pay cuts. The second filed Chapter Eleven. Then Thirteen. The lighted marquis on the front of the entrance quickly changed names, and I found myself working for a third employer. Although the employees stayed the same, the merchandise, president, and regional managers soon changed. There was nothing that could shock me about the accelerated transformations of my California world.

During those first years I had candidly read every book on launching a new business and prepared a plan. I was convinced that I could establish a jewelry company that would flourish and attract customers from everywhere. I also remembered the shortcomings and business mistakes of my former employers and scribbled many do's and don't's in my binder.

While saving a portion of my paychecks from previous years, I always calculated the possibilities of opening a business. After much thought, I sold what was left of my music equipment to raise more capital. I created spreadsheets on my computer, attended seminars, and vigorously read books of the trade even while basking on the beach with Carmen. Every book returned to the library would bear smudged pages from suntan oil.

I secretly corresponded with companies that, as a whole, are responsible for making the business prosper. In a painful decision to become economically independent, I said good-bye to my employer. I subdued my feelings about the likelihood of failure, and I was at the same time exhilarated realizing that this would be a still newer era in my life.

It was only two years since I first unloaded the Ryder truck in Santa Ana, and now I was already planning on being self-employed. Because I had invested every dollar into the new venture, the unwelcome thought of losing everything I owned haunted me deliriously. At a predetermined date marked on the calendar, I signed a lease, installed a safe, showcases, and overhead lighting, and displayed a Grand Opening advertisement in the newspaper. On September 15, 1991, *Gallery of Diamonds* was christened in Costa Mesa.

Since I had so vividly constructed a jewelry company in my dreams, it was almost as if I had already worked there for many years. I played the multiple roles of manager, merchandiser, and of course, salesperson. Carmen worked equally hard painting, cleaning, and making sure the wall hangings were placed perfectly. My brain was so filled with the fierce battle of sales projections verses overhead expenses that there was no room left for wondering about my biological beginnings.

September was a strategic time to open a jewelry business, I deducted, for it allowed three months of market penetration before the fury of holiday shoppers. Although the grand opening produced lower than projected sales, shoppers began to trickle into the store during the following months.

The unpredictable future prevented me from getting much sleep during those early times. I would have nightmares seeing the letters of my Grand Opening banner transfiguring themselves into, "Going Out of Business." Nevertheless, my once nearly eradicated bank account finally rose to a comfortable level. And although Gallery of Diamonds never saw a "fury" of holiday shoppers during its first Christmas, it soon snugly positioned itself in the jewelry market for loose diamonds and wedding and engagement jewelry.

On July 23, 1993, I married Carmen. I adored her more than any girl I had ever met and realized that it had taken me a former love and a former spouse to lead me to her. We had a small ceremony in Laguna Beach, overlooking the Pacific Ocean. Our wedding photo was taken on the majestic crags that protrude from the crashing waves. Her dress gleamed bright in the sun. And because we had always spent so much precious time together walking and talking on the wet sand, I still think of my Carmen when I see the ocean.

Tu eres mi oceano
Tu eres mi luna
Maria del Carmen

16. *Lady By The Lake*

Three months after Carmen and I were married I made the final attempt to discover my origins. During a quiet moment at the store, I referred back to the original court summary and read it again from behind the cluttered papers on my desk. My mind rewound ten years when I shared the summary with my parents in our living room. Noblesville had always been a physical place on the map. Plymouth, however, was always mysterious to me, quite possibly contrived as the city my birthmother was from, and it was even more obscure now that I lived nearly two thousand miles away from it. Then again, I was angry at myself for not attempting to explore this area earlier in my life.

I spoke to a newspaper editor from Plymouth. It must have been a small town hungry for news because a week later the newspaper displayed on its first page, "Watson Searches for Mother." There was a photo of myself that I had sent along with a few hand-written paragraphs and concluded with my work telephone number.

This time somebody called.

"Is this Michael Watson?" an elderly and faraway voice asked.

"Yes, that's me."

"My name is Margy Flora and I read the article in this morning's paper, and I just wanted to say that I knew your birthmother."

My heart jumped. "Y...you did?"

"Now she's not living anymore, I'm sorry to say, but I just want you to know that Betty Price was a very fine lady. We went to school together many years ago. At our last class reunion, she was listed as deceased, but I wanted to send you a photo of her taken by the lake. I will send it to you so you will know what she looked like."

"You really knew her?"

"Oh yes, dear. I'm going to send you this picture so you will always remember your birthmother as the beautiful lady by the lake."

"How old is she, I mean, *was* she?"

"I don't know when she passed away. She was a year younger than me. So she would have been seventy-three years old now."

I raised an eyebrow and twisted my mouth towards the left side of my face. I knew this warmhearted lady was getting ready to send a photo of another Betty Price, for if she would have been seventy-three than I would have miraculously aged sixteen years. Nevertheless, I gave her my address and two days later I received a black and white photo of an attractive lady posing in front of what seemed more like a duck pond. It wasn't my mother. That's the last I heard from anyone in Plymouth.

Southern California had been deluged with every catastrophe known, including earthquakes, fires, floods, and riots. Although I had personally escaped each danger, I could not escape the peril of my own biological ignorance. I realized I had made an isolated journey to the point of no return. The desire to know my blood roots was far beyond a curiosity. It now consumed me.

I heard of a service that, for a small fee, would generate a computer listing of any name in the United States. I sent my check and three days later I received a four-page report of over three hundred and fifty Michael Prices in the country. One of those Michaels, I had hoped, would be my half-brother. Finding him would not only be an easier task, but it would also be the key to finding my birthmother. I made a few hundred copies of the court summary I had guarded like a precious gem and included this form letter in my mass mailing:

October 30, 1993

Dear Mr. Price,

Please look over the enclosed copy of the court summary. I was adopted in 1958. I have never known my birthmother, father, half-brother, or anyone in my natural family. The reason I am writing you is because there is a possibility that you could be related to me.

Please read the section that says "MOTHER OF CHILD." If your mother's name was Betty Price or if there are any names, dates, or places that are familiar to you, please call me collect.

Thank you for your help. I have been searching for members of my natural family my entire life. If nothing sounds familiar, please pass this on to someone else in your family.

I neatly folded the letters and inserted them into about two hundred envelopes. When the mailman noticed that all were addressed to Mr. Michael Price, he shrugged his shoulders, shook his head, then stashed them under his arm as he left in a bewildered state.

I waited patiently for return mail or telephone calls. Maybe my half-brother received the letter but thought the whole thing was a prank, or perhaps didn't want to reveal himself.

A Michael Price with a pronounced southern drawl called on the third day. Because the jewelry store was busy I put him on hold and promised to return immediately. After what seemed like several minutes, I returned and thanked him for hanging on. He then proceeded to tell me that he received my letter but was sorry that he was in no way related to me. Not only was that the wrong answer, I was also aggravated because he was calling collect from nine hundred miles away. I thanked him but nevertheless replaced the receiver with a harder than average force.

For You created and shaped me
Gave me life within my mother's womb
For the wonder of who I am I praise you
Safe in your hands, all creation is made new

17. *The Mystery Clue*

A recent amendment in Indiana allowed adoptees and birthparents to complete a form from the State Department of Health, the *Indiana Adoption History Registration*, which would give consent for the searching parties to exchange identifying or non-identifying information. I remembered that I had sent that form one year ago and also that I had not received a reply. Either my birthmother did not want to find me, she was dead, or she wasn't familiar with such a service. I hoped for the latter.

I felt I had tried every conceivable method of searching by using the information I derived, other than paying a private detective, which I stubbornly refused.

At home I fetched a folder that I had always kept in a locked file and burrowed through the myriad of papers that I had toted with me for most of my life. Inside lay the barely legible notes from the calls I had made at the elderly couple's house on North Delaware Street. Also were the phone numbers of three erroneous Michael Prices I resisted throwing away. I remembered there was one Michael Price that I must have called at least three times in my life. The last time I called he said, 'You're the one that's searching for your mother, aren't you?'

I clutched the two postcards of Community Hospital, each being twenty years apart, and also the three, wrinkled blue folders Mom had given me as a child.

I cautiously read every word of the court summary. Carmen fell asleep beside me as I continued reading. I memorized every word.

The next morning I took an out-of-the-way route to the store. For security reasons, frequently changing one's driving routine is a good idea for anyone in the jewelry business. While driving I remembered an independent search consultant once told me to voice my opinions about opening up sealed adoption records to legislators. When I arrived, I retrieved a name from somewhere in the cosmos of my computer's hard drive and began to type.

March 29, 1994

Health and Human Services Director
The White House
Washington, D.C 20500

I am an adoptee. I love my adoptive parents more than one can imagine. However, I feel this same emptiness that most adoptees feel. Where did I come from? Who am I? Is there a medical disorder in my family I should know about?

Fourteen years ago, after much persistence, I received a copy of the court summary of my adoption. Although it has led me on an unsuccessful journey, this information could be the key for thousands of adoptees to live their lives knowing the truth about their heritage and meeting another human being that physically resembles them.

I earnestly ask you, let's open up the sealed records. I will continue to search for my natural mother, father, and members of my family until my death. I also speak for the multitude of America's adoptees: We just want to know the truth.

I received a belated reply that only claimed the person I addressed the letter to was no longer the Health and Human Services Director.

Later that day I called the city county building in Indianapolis. Other than making three previous trips I believe this was the first time I had ever *called* them.

I asked the clerk if they had any more information other than the court summary. I will never forget the dialogue that took place.

"What form are you referring to?" the lady who answered asked.

"It says, court docket number five dash three three seven. And underneath, 'Case number E-38-02892,'" I answered, reading the top of the document.

"How did you get that form?" the lady demanded.

"Judge Jameson gave it to me when I came to your office when I was about twenty-three."

"You're not supposed to have that form," she said sternly, and then I wondered if she expected me to mail it back. She continued to say that another judge had taken Judge Jameson's place and that they were very strict about releasing information.

I hung up. Although I had been dawdling at a dead end for the past nineteen years, I felt blessed to own a trace of genealogical evidence that many adoptees are refused.

That evening I questioned for the first time if Noblesville was only a place my birthmother purported to be from to ensure that I would never find her. As a result of this line of thought, I commenced a personal expedition to find her wedding license application. Although I had previously failed at that endeavor, I never had queried anywhere other than Marion or Hamilton counties. I retrieved the addresses of every Indiana courthouse from some resource books and discovered that there were close to a hundred other counties in the state.

The next morning I typed the short request in duplicate.

Good morning,

Please search and send a copy of the marriage license application for:
WHO: Floyd Price and Betty _____ (maiden name unknown)
WHEN: Approximately December 29, 1951.
If cannot find, please check between years of 1951-1956.
If there is a charge for this service, please let me know.

Fifty pages spewed out white and crisp from my printer. I spent most of the morning dividing them with a pair of scissors and then neatly stuffed, stamped, and rubberbanded them into a generic white pile before the mailman arrived.

My request was identical from many years ago except that I would be expanding my market one-hundred-fold to the rest of Indiana. My scheme was that if I failed in my home state, I would continue mass marketing letters to every single courthouse in the United States if necessary.

Three weeks later I went to the store early to fill some jewelry orders. I had also been besieged with mail that was left unopened from the previous busy day. As I sorted them into three piles of bills, account payments, and junk mail, I found three letters from Indiana courthouses. I was not a novice at receiving rejection letters, and I vowed never to get my hopes up for anything that was given to me from a mail carrier. Nevertheless, I used my right thumb as a letter opener and yanked out the contents of each envelope.

During the previous weeks I had been sent copies of many irrelevant wedding license applications from different counties, none of which seemed to have any significance with my genesis. But the third envelope with a return address of Putnam County stirred my attention, for the headline read, "Application is hereby made for a License for the Marriage of: Floyd Price to Betty Stewart." As I veered downwards, the issue date was December 29, 1951 -- the precise wedding date mentioned in the court summary.

The shock of seeing a statistical match caused me to feel weak. It would be much easier to regard the incident as a hoax, I thought, but the coincidence was too obvious. Along with the lifelong habit of searching, I had become comfortable in accumulating erroneous information. It was uncomfortable, however, to once again hold a document in my hands that was somehow associated with my introduction to this world.

I held the Z-folded record open at arms length and viewed it like a student who was studying abstract art for the first time. The blanks were filled in with exaggerated spirals and words that were slanted to the right. Because of my own left-handedness, my writing slanted in the opposite direction. The first letter of each word was strongly accented followed by much smaller lowercase letters. Small p's, g's, and y's sometimes looped down three or four lines. I deducted that it was a young female that filled out the entire parchment, and I was overwhelmed by the certainty of seeing my birthmother's penmanship for the first time. The style of the handwriting was my first glimpse into her creative past. If my search had truly come to an end, I tried to convince myself to feel fortunate in possessing an artifact that so many adoptees are denied, like the handwriting swirls of one's birthmother that float on the surface of a piece of paper.

I looked again at the name of the future bride on the top right corner. Her maiden name was Stewart. The application was divided into two columns for each applicant: left for the male, right for the female. I peered down the right column and continued reading. In thc blank asking the full Christian and surname of father was written Otis Stewart. His occupation said state highway employee. My Grandfather! Until that moment I had never conceptualized another grandpa, like Mom's dad, who died when I was an adolescent. Grandma died when I was a child. The only thing I remembered about her is instructing me how to put on my undershirt, asserting that the tag must always go in the back.

Further down, specifying the full Christian and maiden name of mother, it said Hattie Murphy. My Grandmother! My personal revelation intensified as I uncovered the identities of three biological relatives.

I scanned for the word Noblesville but it never appeared on the entire page. But filled in the blank, *where born*, was the name of another town with the same suffix -- Coatesville. So that's where she was from! I involuntarily made a quick turn as if to tell somebody the news until I realized I was the only one there. Then I became cognizant of standing alone in the mortal silence. The whir of computer hard drives, fax machines, and the rumble of the jewelry polisher had not yet commenced. Hurling towards my desk, I fetched the only map of the United States at hand. It was a pocket-sized one and showed only the major cities.

I called my next door neighbor, Randy Clayton. Randy was a genius in world geography and owned a computer with lightning speed access to almost any place on the globe. I told him about my discovery and asked him to look up Coatesville on the Internet. After pressing a few keys he said it was a very small town about thirty miles west of Indianapolis and had a current population of three hundred and fifty.

I thanked him, hung up, and fiddled with the application for several minutes. Then I called Carmen who was still at home. I stuttered my excitement into the tiny holes of the mouthpiece and hung up without saying Good-bye.

Then I called Mom. Other than the physical act of giving birth to me, she had not only been my mother in every sense of the word but also my friend. As her telephone rang I hoped that the combined words intermingled in my mouth and brain would be delivered coherently. For a brief second I realized the ridiculousness of saying, 'Hi, mother, I found my mother.'

She picked up on the third ring. "Mom, I found my birthmother!" I blurted triumphantly.

"What do you mean, you *found* her?" She spoke firmly, but dazed.

"Her name was Betty Stewart. That was her maiden name." Then I realized that it would be impossible for her to share my excitement, at least at the same intensity as myself. As I waited for her response, I also realized that this victorious day for me might have also been the day she has dreaded since I was born. I proceeded to tell her about my morning's mail.

"Stoy, honey, Michael found his birthmother," she spoke with a monotone toward Dad's chair. Dad's muffled voice echoed from the background. "What are you going to do now, I mean, just be careful, Michael, whatever you do."

"I'll let you know as soon as I find out more," I answered. "After all, this information is forty-three years old. I might not *find* anyone. I love you."

"I love you, too. Just be careful. Good-bye."

I could not concentrate on the jewelry business the entire day. I was certain that this particular piece of mail would be the key that would unlock the vaulted door to my obscure past. I felt driven to journey to Coatesville by plane or by foot, but gradually composed myself and tried to allow logic to take the place of my emotions. I had waited far too long, I thought, to allow all my years of genealogical exploration to become vain.

I had heard of a Master Death file, a retrieval system in which one can verify if an individual has died. I never had a use of such a service before, realizing that my birthmother's last name would have surely changed. Or maybe it was because I was afraid that she very well may be dead. I made a quick pencil calculation and ascertained that she would presently be fifty-nine.

I had somehow acquired the telephone number of a researcher that had access to death records in Indiana. After opening the address file from my computer, I dialed the number. I told the answerer the information she requested: which were the names, Otis and Hattie Stewart; the town, Coatesville; and a parameter of possible dates of death.

The rapid pecking of the researcher's fingers on her computer keypad sounded like Morse Code on seventy-eight speed. "No one listed as Hattie Stewart, sir," she responded. My heart drummed when I realized that my grandmother must still be alive.

"Let me try Otis Stewart." The pecking continued. "I have three listings for O. Stewart," the researcher said. "And, yes,...*tapk tapk*...here we are,...*tapk*, Stewart, Otis died in Coatesville, Indiana in May, 1987." She spoke without emotion or remorse. Of course, it was not her job to console mourners. To her I was just an everyday caller, pursuing the archives of the past. She had no idea that the persons I was searching for were the biological grandparents I had never met and that I never knew existed before I opened this mornings mail.

I felt ill. I had already begun to visualize my grandfather as a hardworking citizen who was likable to all who met him, and now he was dead. As far as I was concerned, he had died right there as I held the telephone receiver against my ear.

"The charge is ten dollars," she said, interrupting my train of thought. "Please mail me a check, and I will send you a full report."

I obeyed by involuntarily reaching for my checkbook after I replaced the receiver. My grandfather had died seven years ago, and I had never even met him.

At closing I went home and carefully handed Carmen the document as if it were one of the Dead Sea Scrolls. I reread the notes in my personal files to confirm I had really found my blood family. Everything matched except the name of the town. It now seemed certain that my birthmother intended to camouflage her trail, for Coatesville was located many miles on an opposite side of Indianapolis. I had been searching in the wrong place for the past twenty years.

Carmen and I reviewed the application from the living room sofa. The phone rang.

"Michael, did you find out anything else?" Mom said.

"No, Mom. Except that my grandfather is dead," I answered.

"What do you mean, your grandfather's dead?" she asked, confused. I proceeded to explain.

"Honey, me and your daddy have been looking on the map, and we can't find Coatesville." At my current age of thirty-six, I still had parents that considered themselves as my mommy and daddy. "There is one place that looks like...C.T.S.V." I could tell she was straining her eyes as she pronounced each letter "...but I don't see no Coatesville."

"That's it, Mom. It's a very small town, smaller than its own name."

"You're not going there...to Coatesville...are you?" Like all moms, I suppose mine knew me more than anyone else on earth, and she also knew that no city would stand between me and my endless quest.

"No, Mom. Don't worry. How do we even know anyone's still living there?" I heard her sigh with relief, and we bade each other goodnight. Then I realized what I had just said. I wondered if anyone genetically related to me actually did still live in a town in which the population totaled less than half the amount of units in my Californian apartment complex. Although I never considered myself nomadic, I had lived in three states and several cities in the past thirty-six years. It was more likely, I imagined, that my biological family had probably already drifted to the ends of the earth.

18. *Journey To The Black Hole*

Waking early, I went to the store before the sun rose. It was a dangerous move that I have since not made, for security reasons it is vital that more than one person opens or closes a jewelry store. Nevertheless, I relocked the door behind me and notified the alarm company of my early arrival. I flipped on the Mr. Coffee and carried the copy of the marriage license application to my leather chair.

I had never taken anyone's advice on hiring a private investigator, and now *I* was masquerading as one. Betty Price had finally been identified as the former Betty Stewart. If I had known her maiden name twenty years ago, I would have surely called every Stewart in the phone books of my past. I realized how fruitless it was to mangle my fingers from the old rotary phone from the elderly couple's home on North Delaware Street.

After swallowing a hard, first gulp, I was struck by what seemed to be a brilliant idea. Since I knew the date of my grandfather's death, all I had to do was find the obituary in the local newspaper. It would most likely list the survivors, including my birthmother, and also state where they were currently living. I pushed a couple of numbers on my calculator and found that Betty would have been fifty-one at that time. If I could read an obituary column, it would reveal her current married name. The most recent data I had ever uncovered about her, according to my worn court summary, was 'on September 15, 1955, she divorced Mr. Price.' Surely she would have remarried during the succeeding four decades. Quite possibly more than once.

My mind scrambled to devise a way to get a copy of a Coatesville local paper. I knew the month and year Otis passed away, but the researcher had no record of the exact day. At least I wouldn't have to thumb through more than thirty-one papers, if it was indeed a daily publication. I imagined the column saying something like: "...and Otis Stewart is also survived by his daughter, Betty Johnson, who now resides with her husband, Tom, in Phoenix, Arizona."

I could just call information for Coatesville and get the name of the local paper. Maybe it was released weekly. But what if there were no copies of the papers? Surely the old publications would not be computerized. Coatesville was not like New York, for heaven's sake. Although the data I was seeking was only seven years old, a town that minuscule might not religiously preserve the written records of its past. My mind rambled as I noticed myself creating my own obstacle course. After all, I was convinced that nothing in this world was easy or free. The notion of speaking to the editor of the Coatesville newspaper was too obvious, and like the hopeless odds of winning the lottery, I never remembered obtaining anything of value from a simple phone call.

A scrolled piece of paper lay on the floor. It was a fax from Randy Clayton who must have sent it during the night. Uncurling it, I read the headline: 'Coatesville Community Development Association. Welcome To Our Community.' Randy had apparently conducted further research on the small town.

> The town of Coatesville originated sometime during the early 1850's. It was incorporated in 1909 and two years later the town built a school house.
>
> Coatesville was originally a village called West Milton. However, an early settler by the name of Henry Coates gave some

> land for the town site and because of his liberal offering the town was given the name Coatesville.
>
> When the Pennsylvania Railroad was completed, the town soon became a thriving community with a number of businesses ... There was a flour mill where the Elevator now stands, there was a tin and a plumbing shop, four doctor's offices, two saloons, a picture show and numerous smaller businesses.
>
> Coatesville has a very deep Christian heritage. In the early days, there was Methodist, Christian, Baptist, Primitive Baptist, and Quaker churches. All still remain except the Quaker Church.
>
> The town of Coatesville was struck by a tornado on Good Friday, 1948. This was a massive storm that touched down just southwest of Fillmore and lifted off the ground at the west edge of Danville. The business district was devastated. Three of the four churches were destroyed completely.
>
> From the destruction, a new town emerged with merchants and townsfolk of one mind to rebuild...

I fantasized about living in that village. And if it were not for my adoption, I very well might still be there. At least I would have escaped that horrible calamity on Good Friday, which occurred ten years before I was born. I might have been a farmer producing grain or livestock for the populace. I might have had a completely different belief system and religion. My mind ceased to prophesize the possibilities of my fate.

The fax defined my biological homeland as a typical midwestern vicinity. Coatesville was a community that was determined to re-emerge from the barbarous ravages of nature. New Albany had its similar catastrophes, I pondered. The Tornado of 1917 shattered the northwest corner of the city. The Flood of 1937 inundated sixty-five percent of the helpless town. I remembered the horror of the 1976 twister that turned the sky green as I peered from the window of my high school English class.

My adolescent dreams of descending from prestige and wealth disappeared. It was much more likely that my birthparents emanated from a proletarian family rather than a royal one.

I sipped from a second cup of coffee as the sun began to rise. Looking at my watch, I knew that Coatesville was three hours ahead. Then I wondered if my birthmother still lived in that country town. The possibility of the fact did exist. What a preposterous thought, I mused, still struggling between zeal and reason. I reminded myself of my age and almost laughed when I thought of her living in the same house for the past thirty-six years.

Then I stared at my telephone. Maybe the blasphemous ease of merely pushing a few touch tones would put an end to the riddle that has tortured me for two decades. A small town that rested snugly in the heart of swaying corn fields would have midwestern values. The ideologies of the inhabitants were certainly not like those of Southern California, in which one moves to a different dwelling an average of once every three and a half years. There must still be many American communities like Coatesville, I thought, in which the townspeople are born, live, and remain in until they die. My own adoptive parents, for instance, had lived in the same house on Grantline Road for over forty years.

I felt the heaviness of the receiver in my hand as I placed it against my ear. Although my grandfather was dead, my grandmother could still be living there. I dialed information.

"Operator. City, please?" echoed a faint but hurried female voice.

"Uh, Coatesville. Do you have a listing for Stewart, Otis Stewart in Coatesville?" I was completely prepared for the response, 'Sorry, sir, no listing.' I was stunned, however, by the actual reply that resounded into my ear.

"Hold for the number, please," and then a computer artificially blared a series of numerals. "The number is...7-6-4-0-8-5-2."

I grabbed a pen from a far corner on my desk.

"Repeat... 7-6-4-0-8-5-2." The audio digitized numerals bellowed evenly spaced and without gender. I managed to scrawl the numbers onto a piece of paper and then replaced the receiver numbly. I stared at my hardly legible characters. Although Otis had passed away several years ago, there was still a telephone listing. Somebody must still live there! My grandmother? My birthmother?

I fumbled with the wrinkled paper and gaped at the seven digits for twenty minutes. Employees of the shopping center had started to arrive, and the rising sun reflected bright beams from the chrome of their cars. It was now eight o'clock. The jewelry store was not scheduled to open for another two hours.

I realized I was holding the combination to the ancient lock of my past. Maybe a dreadful, horrible past. It had been disguised in seven simple digits. Although I was sure that many adoptees had the ability to invent illusions of grandeur about their birthmothers, I could now only recall the broken phrases from the court summary; "bad dream...too much to drink...not telling the truth."

But what if I found her? The Great Search would be over. Investigating the past had become a very placid and ordinary part-time vocation in my life. The act of *finding,* on the other hand, involved swinging a machete through uncharted territory. I was terrified. I then remembered those precious moments with Carmen when I assured her that there was nothing in life to be afraid of; the fear of storms, the fear of failure, the fear of darkness. I felt that I had personally overcome all of my own adolescent fears, but then I noticed one that unrelentingly returned to torment me - the fear of the Unknown.

The seven digits stared back at me from the wrinkled surface of business stationery. The silhouette of the diamond logo shone through from the other side. I caressed the paper, being cognizant of the delicate texture between my fingers. The numbers were to my "home," in a newly defined sense. Like the numbers of one's street address or current age that is eternally memorized as a child, they would have been seven digits as deeply instilled in my brain as the date of my birth.

There was no sense in calling Mom again or Carmen either. I had to push the numbers on the telephone keypad. I dialed '1,' then the area code, then the remainder of the seven digits.

Except the last one.

Then I replaced the receiver. What would I say, for God's sake? I persecuted myself in composing my first words. What if my birthmother answered? Or my grandmother? I began to pen a fictitious dialogue on another piece of paper. Surely the answerer would think I was a psychopath.

Then I was overcome by a strange, familiar, almost sickening feeling. I mentally returned to the day of my youth when I stood alone, freezing to death in front of that lone house on Featheringill Road. I prayed that someone would answer. But just as soon as I was acknowledged, the door was then shut again. If the lady had not let me inside her warm hearth, I surely would have died that morning in the bitter cold.

Perhaps that is what would happen all over again. I would call this number, and once the answerer heard my introduction would say, "I'm sorry, sir. You must have the wrong number. I've never heard of a Betty Price. Good-bye." Perhaps I had indeed found the door that would solve the riddle of my past. But after the contents would be briefly revealed, it would then reseal itself in a tighter defense, like a land turtle that locks itself in its shell. The pages of the past could be sucked into a Black Hole.

But I didn't die that morning on Featheringill Road, and I would be given a chance, nearly twenty years later to find out where I came from.

I re-dialed the number, including the last digit. The faint ring came from a planet outside my familiar solar system. An elderly lady answered.

"Hello?" she said.

"Hello. Is this Hattie Stewart?"

"Yes." I was thrilled and terrified on hearing the voice of another human being that shared the same DNA as myself.

"My name is Michael Watson. I'm calling you from California. Was your daughter's name Betty, who got married to a Floyd Price?" I already knew those answers, but I wanted to interject something personal, something that only a friend or relative could know, something that would arrest her attention before she slammed the receiver in my ear.

"Yes."

"Mrs. Stewart, I don't know how to tell you this, but your daughter, Betty, is my biological mother. I was adopted in 1958 after I was born in Community Hospital in Indianapolis."

Although I wanted to scream that sentence, I restrained myself. Each word was paced evenly with the same volume.

"Who is this?" she asked skeptically.

I repeated my words once more.

"I'm very sorry," she said. I braced myself for what was coming next. But instead, she answered differently. "My daughter had a boy named Michael, but he was born in 1953."

"Yes, I know!" I said. "Michael David Price. I found out about him many years ago. My name happens to be Michael also, but I was named by my adoptive parents."

"Now hold on there," she continued with concern. "Betty had another child, but he was stillborn."

"I'm very sorry, Ma'am," I said apologetically. "When did that happen?"

"It was in February. In 1958."

"I'm very sorry," I repeated. Then I came to my senses. "*I* was born in February of 1958. That's me!" I spoke wildly. Then after using all my energy to constrain my excitement I said, "I am certainly not dead, and *you* are my natural grandmother!"

There was numbing silence. I pressed the receiver hard against my ear. Five seconds passed. I noticed I was now standing. I strained to hear. She was not speaking. Perhaps she was waiting for me to speak again. Ten seconds. I lost track of time. Perhaps she had been swallowed by the Black Hole. Then she spoke.

"You know," she paused, "we always wondered if you were really alive."

"What do you mean, *alive*, Mrs. Stewart?" I said. "Didn't Betty, your daughter, tell you that she put me up for adoption?"

"Betty always told us that you were stillborn, but we always wondered if you were alive."

"Yes. I'm *very much* alive," I said. And before I could absorb the fact that I had gone down in the annals of the Stewart lineage as being deceased, I said, "Please tell me about Betty. I have been trying to find her since I was a teenager."

"She had a very hard life," she answered.

And then I wondered why a mother would begin a description of her own daughter in such negative terms. I would not settle for such a vague answer. Even the court summary painted a more complete picture of her.

"What does she look like, Mrs. Stewart? Where does she live?" I pleaded.

"Betty passed away thirteen years ago," she spoke regretfully.

I felt my right leg tremble. I braced myself on my desk with my free arm. "What do you mean, *she passed away?"*

"She died in 1981 in Quincy, Massachusetts, but I guess you still have many uncles, aunts, and cousins here in Coatesville."

Something inside told me that I should have wept. After all, my birthmother had died, and like my grandfather Otis, was murdered at that very instant. But I didn't cry. It didn't make sense, chronologically anyway, that I was speaking to my grandmother, yet my birthmother had already passed away thirteen years ago.

"How did she die?" I asked.

"Cirrhosis of the liver."

"Did she drink?" I asked reflexively.

"Yes. She had a very hard life," she repeated.

During the next moments I explained how I derived her telephone number and gave a brief synopsis of my life, my adoptive parents, and my wife. I told her that I wanted nothing personal from her, only to know where I came from. She seemed to listen with a close ear and uttered what sounded like a closing statement, "Well, I guess I'll tell the rest of the family that they now have relatives in California."

I felt the conversation coming to an end. My birthmother was dead. Even I was dead. And now this brief and frail alien encounter would perhaps be my first and last contact with the other world. I squeezed the receiver.

"Can I call them?" I said. "I mean, don't you think they should know about me?"

"I'll let them know," she said. "I feel it would be better for me to tell the rest of the family." The conclusion of our first and possibly only interchange was nearing. I was afraid to hang up. I was sickened to hear of my birthmother's death. I was enthralled to realize that I had a biological *family*. My emotions were so tangled that I felt as if half of my body had been immersed in freezing water while the other half was boiling.

I couldn't just keep the phone to my ear, I thought. I believed she was waiting for me to say good-bye first, after all, I was the one who called. "It was a pleasure talking to you, Mrs. Stewart." Although she was actually my grandmother, it would have been awkward to address her as such. "Good-bye."

"Bye, now."

The telephone was still cemented to my ear. Then before a second passed, I blurted, "Mrs. Stewart?"

"Yes." She was still there. I felt ill. Not only had I been dead for the past thirty-six years, but my birthmother had also died. I still hungered to know what she looked like. There was the possibility that Mrs. Stewart might not want to make further contact with me again. After all, I was a complete stranger, for no one in the Coatesville universe even knew of my existence.

"Mrs. Stewart," I repeated, "Why don't I send you a picture of myself and my wife and my adoptive parents, and then maybe you could send me a picture of Betty and yourself."

"That would be fine," she answered. We exchanged addresses, bid farewell, and proceeded to hang up once again.

"Mrs. Stewart!" I cried again as I pulled the receiver back to my mouth.

"Yes."

"This might be a silly question, but what nationality are you, was Betty, am *I*? I mean, you see, I don't know who or what I am."

"Well, we're all-American," she said.

That was not the answer I expected. Mrs. Stewart did continue to explain that no one knew who my birth father was, who apparently rendered my Mediterranean traits. "Well, I'm definitely not *all-American*," I responded, "but I'm looking forward to getting your pictures in the mail."

We bid adieu for the third time and hung up.

A lot of ground was covered during those primal moments. Hattie Stewart said her husband died in 1987. I told her I was sorry and didn't mention I learned that from a computer researcher. She spoke of my mother's sister and brothers -- my aunts and uncles. She told me their names -- Mary Jane, David, Bob. She spoke of Michael David, and another younger brother, Kenny Ray. I had another brother!

She mentioned Suzie. A sister! And she spoke sadly of Debra Kay, another sibling who disappeared. She had vanished before her second birthday. Betty apparently wasn't able to provide a singular explanation, saying to some that a baby sitter had stolen her and to others that a social worker took her.

I felt her grief as we spoke, for Debra Kay was a little girl that everyone knew and loved, and then suddenly she disappeared from the face of the earth. I, on the other hand, was not a tragedy, but merely a child that suffered the unfortunate circumstances of being born dead.

I remember straining to hear every muttered word about the secrets of the past. Michael David was the first child born in 1953, then Debra Kay, then me, then Suzie, and Kenny Ray. I had two brothers and two sisters!

The next morning I typed her a letter, trying to veil my excitement.

June 9, 1994

Dear Hattie,

It was so nice to hear your voice. I am 36 and that was the first time I have ever spoken to anyone that was a biological relative. I have searched for Betty Price since I was seventeen. I feel sad that I will never have a chance to meet her.

I am sending you a copy of the court summary that I received many years ago along with the application of the marriage license of Betty and Floyd that I recently received. This is what led me to you.

I am also sending pictures of myself and my wife. She is a very beautiful and caring person.

I was blessed with wonderful adoptive parents who continue to live in New Albany, where I lived most of my life.

I would like to meet you one of these days and all of my relatives who would like to meet me also. Please send me pictures of my birthmother. I've wondered what she looked like my entire life. It has never concerned me about why I was put up for adoption, but I have always been curious about where I came from.

Your grandson.

The following two weeks went by painfully slow, for I had not heard another word from her. I knew that mail from Indiana to California took no more than a few days. My grandmother had professed to being eighty-four years old, and her voice lacked vitality. Perhaps she had gotten sick, or decided against mailing me any photos. Maybe she was finally at peace in knowing of my existence and decided not to let the secret venture further. Perhaps she had died.

Twice I almost called again, but now it was her turn to contact me. It was *someone's* turn to contact me, I protested to myself. After all, *I* was the one who had been searching for nearly twenty years. Couldn't someone just pick up the phone and call me?

The mailman came. The return address was from Coatesville. The envelope appeared scrawled over several times, with slight variations of my address, as if the letter was continuously returned to the sender for lack of my correct address. I opened the envelope and dove straight to the enclosed photo. It was an outdoor scene with an attractive dark-headed girl standing next to an older woman. From the date underneath the weathered polaroid, I knew the elder woman must have been my mother, and that the picture was taken just a few years before she died. I strained to see a frail resemblance of myself through the blurry snapshot. Then I realized that the younger girl was my sister, Suzie. She must have been around seventeen, and for the first time I encountered a reflection of myself in the photograph of another human.

I had stayed in frequent contact with my grandmother, calling her at least once a week. And, like an archeologist who carefully brushes away the dirt that conceals ancient mysteries, I probed her for more and more pieces of my biological past.

Mom seemed strangely calm about my discovery, and I wondered if it was because her biggest adversary had vanished. Did her sudden burst of support emerge from the fact that the unknown enemy, my birthmother, had died?

Nevertheless, I was proud of my breakthrough and made sure Mom and grandmother had each other's addresses and telephone numbers.

19. *The Reunion*

Labor Day was approaching. Carmen and I had practically lived at our jewelry company for the previous four years and had abstained from taking a needed vacation. I missed my parents awfully. We decided to close the business for a week and fly to Indiana. Mom said Coatesville was only three hours by car, so I could invite Hattie Stewart and any other interested parties to come to New Albany. That was a brilliant idea. For if that gathering did take place, I would want my parents to be there with me.

I took her advice, called my grandmother, and expressed my wishes. She agreed to come "if the Good Lord was willin."

September 4, 1994. It was a hot Sunday, the day before Labor Day. Carmen and myself had arrived in Indiana and were enjoying my parents' company. The flight from the night before seemed long, but our exhaustion was rejuvenated as we anticipated our new guests in the late morning. From telephone interchanges with my grandmother, Mom said Hattie was coming for sure, along with my birthmother's sister and brother.

Then I heard tires slowly crackling against the dry limestone gravel of the driveway. Two cars had wheeled in front with the sound of apprehension, as when one realizes he or she might be at the wrong address. I was certain, however, who the visitors were.

I rushed outside. The next thing I remember is standing defenselessly in the center of the yard, peering into each of the car's windows. There were six passengers, four in one car and two in the other. They were also staring at me. I realized I was standing alone and felt naked. My mind was dazed, but I believe the first person out of one of the cars was my grandmother. I recognized her from the photo she sent of her and Otis's fiftieth anniversary. She approached me and opened her arms calling me *grandson*. I hugged her reflexively.

Then I saw a younger woman with fluffy, brownish hair, with somewhat the same texture as my own. She lacked any trace of a smile and deliberately approached me as if I were a harmless, yet unknown animal species.

The woman was Mary Jane, Aunt Mary Jane. She reached for my hands with a firm squeeze and peered deep into my eyes, studying me with scientific curiosity. I yearned for similarity. We were both speechless standing under the warm, September sun.

Then I was dizzily transported back to that unremembered time of my birth. The past rammed into the present with immense velocity. I felt I was dreaming, but the cool grasp of her hands was real. The pages of my book of life flipped backwards at the speed of light. The woman's voice and smile finally broke my semi-conscious state, exclaiming that she just wanted to make sure I was really her sister's son.

The front yard become more and more filled with people. Carmen came from behind me. Then Mom and Dad. Then the other occupants of the two vehicles. I later imagined what the neighbors thought as they looked outside to see ten people standing equidistantly, silently staring at one another, as if waiting to be asked to dance.

Other than Hattie, the guests admitted their fear of coming, for they believed the whole ordeal could have been a hoax. After Hattie told me that I wasn't supposed to be alive, I understood their feelings, for I must have been like some kind of ghost.

Mom had frequent telephone exchanges with my grandmother and gave her a warm embrace, like she was an old friend. Then she ushered everyone into the living room. I walked from stranger to stranger saying, "So you must be my___?" filling in the blanks with aunt, uncle, etc, while shaking their hands in a polite, businesslike manner. During those first moments I had met two uncles, two aunts, a first cousin, and my Grandmother Hattie. Even Dad conversed with the new visitors like he had known them all of his life.

I scanned the new faces searching for physical similarity. We compared eyes, noses, ears, and receding hair lines. No one, however, was the spitting image of myself. The new guests later said that neither of them knew my biological father. And like my grandmother stated, everyone indeed looked *all-American.* There was nothing unusual or supernatural about anyone.

The aroma of Mom's pot roast permeated the house. The kitchen table was a place I had always fondly remembered. And now, like an unexpected fantasy, I was sitting down at that table with my parents *and* my biological family.

My name was Jonathan Raymond. At least that was the unofficial name Betty had given me. When she drank heavily, my aunts and uncles remembered her saying that one of these days she was going to find Jonathan Raymond. That confused the family deeply, wondering if I was stillborn or not.

I even told the visitors about the gold-plated amulet I had purchased as a teenager before my first trip to Indianapolis. It was almost twenty years since I had last seen it, and wherever it was I'm sure the inexpensive metal had long become oxidized from the dampness of my parents' house.

When we drifted to the subject of Betty, the ambience of the kitchen grew somber, for it seemed that she indeed suffered a difficult life. She began drinking at a tender age and eventually died from the habit only ten years older than my current self. She had married several times, and many of her husbands were afflicted with the same obsession. It was a grisly feeling, realizing that when I was twenty-three years old, sitting in front of Judge Jameson on that jubilant trip to Indianapolis, my birthmother was dying in a hospital in Quincy, Massachusetts.

After finishing a cake which had been swirled with my name, we returned to the living room. Uncle David, my birthmother's brother, had a surprise in the form of a video cassette. Grandmother Hattie and Mom had been in frequent contact, exchanging family photographs. Uncle David created a home video pictorial narrated by Aunt Mary Jane. All ten of us crowded around Mom and Dad's old Zenith as we inserted it into the VCR.

It began with the title, "Michael Watson -- this is your life," and continued with a collage of family photos. Some were very old, as could be noted by the antiquated cars in the background. Some were taken during holidays, some during birthdays. The first photo was my first grade picture. It was a familiar photo that I hadn't seen in a long time and felt a little embarrassed viewing it once again while crowded amongst six strangers. There was a another little girl whose black and white photo was placed beside mine. She appeared to be the same age and displayed my smile and eyes. In fact, notwithstanding her opposite sex, she looked exactly like me, and I immediately thought it was my sister, Suzie.

Uncle David announced the mystery person as Betty.

My biological mother.

The woman who gave birth to me.

It was almost too much to imagine that I entered this world through the womb of the innocent girl that I was viewing on the twenty-five inch screen. When I finally came to my senses I wondered how many people actually possess a photograph of their mothers when they were in the first grade.

Frame by frame, there was at least one of the visitors who had something to say about a particular photo, for it would conjure up memories of when someone went to the Marine Corps, when someone had a baby, got married, had a heart attack, or passed away.

The complete Stewart lineage was on that tape. There was one photo of Grandmother Hattie as a young girl with *her* mother, father, and siblings. And then there was my great-great grandfather James Murphy from Blacksberry, Kentucky, posing proudly with a large hat, double breasted suit and a cane.

Some of our neighbors had also found close seats by our old console. The reunion was equally exciting for them, for they had known my parents and me since Mom and Dad brought me from Indianapolis. The trunks of everyone's bodies slanted forward sharply, and I imagined that was probably how most Americans were sitting when the assailant of J. R. Ewing was revealed. I don't recall the living room ever being so crowded. I sat semi-Indian style on the crammed floor with my eyes just a few feet from the screen. Mom and Carmen were close to me. Dad eagerly watched from his chair as he gnawed an unlit pipe.

Then there were snapshots of my siblings, Michael David, Kenny Ray, and a high school portrait of Suzie. The next frame was Betty, sitting on someone's front porch with a little baby on her lap. She was quite attractive, wearing a pleasant smile, painted lips and nails, and her hair was fashionably brushed. The baby seemed to be giggling, but the cheerfulness of the room grew solemn when that frame appeared. The baby was my older sister, Debra Kay, and that had been the last photo taken of her since she had vanished. Thoughts of Debra Kay evoked sad memories. She was an innocent child that had yet to manifest her being. In the unrecorded annals of the Stewart genealogy, Debra Kay was a missing person.

When the video was over, the phone rang. Mom answered and passed it to Aunt Mary Jane. She said a few words then re-passed the receiver to me. I hoisted myself from the floor, unaware that my bones weren't as flexible as in my youth.

It was Michael David calling from Florida. He sounded stunned, for although I knew of him for many years, he knew nothing of me until Grandmother Hattie told him shortly after my first telephone call. Although he was my brother, our dialogue was like someone had just introduced us at a formal cocktail party. He briefed me about his life but remembered very little about his own mother, saying that he was raised by Uncle David and his wife. I told him I had been searching for him for a long time and was glad to know that I had a brother. We exchanged telephone numbers and said good-bye.

One person looked at his watch, then the others followed suit lamentably, saying they had to trek back to Coatesville. The word *good-bye* was painful. I believe my own father cried. Like my inability to hang up the telephone during my first contact with my grandmother, it was difficult to accept that the people who shared my bloodline had to leave.

Although my birthmother had passed away many years before, I had finally found my long, lost family. The video was mine to keep. I would share it with my future children. On that day, in the form of magnetic tape, I possessed what millions of adoptees only dream of: their heritage.

As we bid farewell, I addressed the visitors with their new names: Uncle David, Aunt Joy Lee, Uncle Louie, Aunt Mary Jane, *another* Michael, my first cousin, and Grandmother Hattie. It had taken a little practice to form those names with my lips during our first visit, and they echoed back awkwardly into my own ears.

Carmen gathered everyone together outside, and once again we were standing in the front lawn. She quickly lined us up tightly side by side and snapped a photograph. Although I regret that Carmen was not able to be in that photo, I am forever grateful she captured that luminous event.

An amazing thing happened that day. For like a bride and a groom that become a single entity on their wedding day, two families had merged to become one. I still had the same Mom and Dad for the past thirty-six years. That never changed. But now our family consisted of six new members. And before the visitors left, even my own Mom was addressing them with the same prefixes as myself. Even though my grandmother was only a few years older than Mom, she courteously addressed her as "Grandmother" also. Before the evening ended we each had accepted our rightful position in the family hierarchy. My biological family clearly understood that Martha Watson was indeed my mother, the woman who raised and instructed me since day three of my life.

Although my birthmother was dead, I received much more than I had ever asked for. I also wondered if that spectacular event of joyful fellowship could take place in another situation. Before that day there was no common denominator between our two families. Well, one, me. What would happen, I marveled, if one family called upon another in which there was no previous relationship and asked to get together for a reunion? Could that be possible?

20. *Dad*

Carmen and I sat silently in the airplane back to California. I always took the window side, and mostly just gazed at the blanket of clouds below. Sometimes we turned to face each other, sharing a smile and a hand squeeze. The weekend had been like some kind of dream.

A fantastic joy lingered during the weeks and months that passed. Aunt Joy Lee would send letters sometimes twice weekly, filling me in on the archives of the past while expressing the newfound happiness of my Coatesville relatives. I wrote each person also, telling them how thankful I was to find them and that they were able to meet my family. One thing unanimously agreed upon was that the Watson-Stewart Reunion was the event of the century.

Months later I continued to share my success story with every person I met. I had yet to meet my siblings, but had received weekly mail from my *new* aunts and grandmother. Each letter slowly filled in the missing blanks about the life of Betty.

I came to work as usual on Saturday and the answering machine blinked one message. It was Mom, who instructed me to take the next plane back to Indiana, for Dad was in serious condition and was on a breathing machine.

In less than an hour I was strapped inside a 747. Dad had smoked most of his life and still inhaled even when he switched to a pipe. He was diagnosed with emphysema many years ago and now, on top of that, he had pneumonia.

I could never understand why Dad chose to physically ruin himself from alcohol and tobacco. I remembered many persons I had known, including my earlier self, who deliberately destroyed their health. It was difficult to realize how he survived for so many years, and my Mom, who had to breathe each of his smoky exhales.

While peering through the small oval window I remembered that Dad never seemed to show much enthusiasm in any of my school projects or hobbies, thinking that he just wasn't interested. I also remembered him frequently protesting about his difficulty in breathing. Every time I asked what he wanted for his birthday he would just say he wanted to breathe.

Some relatives rushed me from the airport to the hospital. Mom greeted me with a kiss, then began to cry as she prepared me for what I was about to witness. Holding hands, we quietly walked through the double doors marked "Critical Care."

The small room was painted icy green, revealing one little window that separated one from the outside world. Then I saw five elevated bottles of intravenous liquids that cascaded down into my father's body. Thick plastic tubes entered his nostrils and downwards towards his lungs. The only sound one could hear was the amplified sucking of the respirator machine.

"Stoy," Mom said. "Michael's here to see you, honey."

"Hi, Dad," I said, trying to be cheery.

He recognized me and gave a brief smile. Then he continued to look at me. His wrists were bound to prevent him from pulling at the tubes, and since his larynx was blocked it was impossible for him to speak. He released the "call nurse" button to hold my hand. His grasp was weak but felt warm.

The respirator continued to pump life into his lungs. The oxygen level was set at one hundred percent, which was many times the amount one needs to sustain life.

His eyebrows raised and he struggled to lift his upper lip, as if to speak.

"He can't talk," a nurse said that had just appeared from behind me. She wore a pleasant smile and gleamed with sensitivity. Then turning towards Dad, she said, "We know you can't speak with those tubes in your throat, sweetheart. Just relax. You need some rest."

"What does he want?," I asked the nurse.

"Usually they want to be raised up in bed, turned over, or ice to soothe their throat."

"Would you like ice?," I said, hoping for a positive response.

He nodded and I was overjoyed from understanding him. I spooned a tiny cube into his mouth.

He fastened onto the call button once again, as if awaiting for that critical time to press it, perhaps if his pain became intolerable. Then his eyes started to roll back slowly and his lids began to close. When Dad slept I had noticed years ago that sometimes his right eye did not close all the way. I imagined him wandering through time; remembering how he skipped stones across the pond with his brothers, and then advancing through a collage of friends he had garnered from his pipe fitting profession.

Mom patted me on the shoulder and said she was going back to the waiting room. She was tired, and had been there day and night for the last three nights. Just before she left she touched my arm and whispered faintly, "Don't let him see you cry."

The machine inflated his lungs with pure oxygen at slower intervals. "Breathe. Damn it. Breathe!" My brain screamed. I sat beside him and rested my chin on the ice cold bed rail. On that long walk through the corridor Mom told me the doctor said he had a poor chance of making it off the respirator. I began to weep. He reopened his eyes and saw my sadness. I remembered Mom's last words and despised myself, thinking that sorrow was not therapeutic.

He lifted his eyebrows again.

"Ice?," I said, wiping my tears nonchalantly. He shook his head.

"Raised up in bed?," I asked. He shook his head again.

"Turned over?" Wrong again. Then he lifted his hand and appeared to write an invisible word into the air, one letter on top of the other. I shifted my attention between his eyes and hand but could not interpret his message.

Then I grabbed a sketch board I had observed behind me. I unclamped the pencil and folded it in his hand. With his eyes fixed at the ceiling, his trembling hand arduously dragged the graphite across the paper. He had written "Mom". Was he talking about *my* Mom? *His* Mom? Then he looked towards me. Then back to the ceiling. Then towards me.

"I'm sorry, Dad. I know you can't talk. I'll be right back. The nurse will know what you want to say." I couldn't bear thinking what he was trying to express as I ran outside.

The friendly nurse took my sketch board inside the room and returned in five minutes. Her words were evenly paced, serene, and seemed like she had spoken them many times before. "You're father is saying that he is ready to go to heaven."

Then I went to the waiting room. When I saw Mom I cried. She embraced me and said the doctors would now wean him from the machine.

His eyes were half closed as we returned. A nurse wearing the name tag "Alice" injected a clear liquid into the IV, telling us it would help him sleep.

The phone rang early the next morning. It was the friendly nurse, instructing Mom and I to return to the hospital.

When we arrived he was gasping as if he had run several miles. The respirator had now been adjusted to require him to breathe on his own. Over the last few days, the one hundred percent level had been gradually reduced, and now read thirty-five percent. He squirmed uncomfortably.

"We're right here, Dad," I spoke, trying to smooth the opening quiver from my voice. Mom and I grabbed each of his freed hands.

"We're here, honey." Mom said.

The nurse warmly placed her arm around Mom. I'm sure she had seen so many patients die. She looked at her watch every thirty seconds or so and squinted at the monitor above his bed. Her face revealed the grim combination of compassion and realism.

"You're gonna be okay, Dad," I said, kneading his hand. And then I realized that was the first time I ever lied to Dad. He was *not* going to be okay, at least in this physical world. His irises slowly disappeared into his head and he seemed to sway back and forth from the realm of consciousness.

"I love you, Dad," I said, weeping on his hand as I pressed it against my cheek. He reopened his eyes. As we continued to look at each other I was certain that somewhere in his dreamy state his mind struggled to understand, if I truly loved him, why was I letting him die. I turned towards the respirator again. The control panel lights glittered. I was compelled to touch it, adjust it, anything. I could have merely turned the oxygen knob back to fifty or sixty percent and he would be better again.

But I didn't.

The nurse looked back and forth from her wristwatch to the monitor. It was as though she matter-of-factly knew the precise time Dad would pass away.

With Dad's hand against my face I witnessed the vital levels on the monitor plunging. His breathing became slow and shallow. Then the monitor started blinking. The nurse looked at her wrist once more and nodded to Mom.

"He's gone, Michael. He's gone." Mom broke into tears. I gently returned his hand by his side. His call button was still within reach, and although he held on to it for so many days he had never pressed it. Alice returned with a warmed, white blanket and tenderly placed it from his feet to his torso.

When the minister asked me to speak at the funeral, I never imagined a more difficult task. He said I knew my father more than he did. I suppose that was a logical deduction. But I later questioned if I ever knew him at all. Although I loved him we were always constellations apart. My mind was numb. My speech was not prophetic.

I am an adoptee. But even if I had ever met my biological father, Stoy Watson is the only one I could ever call Dad. He loved

> me more than any father could love his natural son. And although we did not share the same physical characteristics, I give him the credit for molding my personality and teaching me the value of loving one's neighbor.
>
> Our lives are short and fragile, and the termination of life may come without any warning. So let this day be a memorial to all to fervently love one another, just like Dad loved all of us.

My biological family that I met only a few months earlier had come once again. I was overjoyed that they had the chance of meeting Dad. But the joy of finding my biological family was in direct proportion to the agony of losing my Dad. Although grief-stricken, I still maintained the belief that everything in life was good and felt that the laws of the universe had somehow intervened once again. And, like the poppy that briefly emerges in the spring and then washes away after the first rain, a new family had been born. There was, I realized, always pain that was associated with birth. The difference was the chronological order.

Before Dad's death my closest family members consisted of Mom, Dad and Carmen. Now I had extended uncles, aunts, a grandparent, and siblings somewhere out there that I would yet meet.

I have forever been grateful for the extra Earth-Time Dad was given to witness the Reunion.

21. *Opening The Files*

There was never a practical or legal use for my original birth certificate. Nevertheless, I always felt it was rightly mine. And even though I had lost the only Dad I had known, I still wondered if the name of my biological father would be revealed.

I re-submitted a request to the Indiana Adoption History division, giving Betty's maiden name. I obeyed the Indiana State Board of Health's recorded telephone directions and enclosed a copy of my drivers license with the correct fee. I expressed needing the certificate soon, saying I was applying for a visa.

This was my condensed reply:

> At this time, all the necessary registration forms have not been received to complete the match. A registration form must be completed by a birthparent and the adoptee to meet the criteria for a match. We can only release your original birth record when we have both consents on file.

I resent a request, this time stating my birthmother had died thirteen years ago.

This was my second reply:

> We are in receipt of an Indiana Adoption History registration form; however, this registration cannot be filled as the form and/

> or entries have been incorrectly completed. We need a copy of the death certificate for Betty Price.
>
> Thank you for your interest.

Reading that letter angered me, for I had to prove that my birthmother died before I could be sent proof that I was even born. It took the death of my biological mother (or, rather the proof that I *knew* she was dead) to obtain the information of my adoption proceedings.

The next week I acquired a copy of Betty's death certificate. It was the first one I had ever seen and it was quite strange that it belonged to the birthmother I had never met. The document was neatly typed and titled, The Commonwealth of Massachusetts, standard certificate of death. It stated her address, recorded her occupation as homemaker, and listed her age at her last birthday as being forty-six. Further down under Place of Disposition said the name of the cemetery she was buried at. The blank for cause of death seemed hurriedly scrawled, saying *Hepatic encephalopathy*, due to a consequence of *Gram negative septicemia*. In layman's terms, Betty Price died from alcohol destruction of her liver and brain.

I sent a duplicate request to the ISDH, but this time with a copy of the death certificate and a hand-written declaration for my unamended birth certificate. Shortly thereafter I received this condensed letter:

> The consents required by IC 31-3-4-28 have been filed in the office of the State Registrar of Vital Records and a written confirmation of the continued desire to participate in the release of information has been received from the registrants. A copy of the Record of Adoption and Certificate of Birth were released on this date to Mr. Michael C. Watson (Adult Adoptee).
>
> Any office or agency holding files pertaining to this proceeding is authorized to release identifying and/or non identifying information to Mr. Michael C. Watson only upon receipt of his request and proper identification. This authorization is not valid unless it carries the raised seal of Indiana.

Agencies Known, Or Believed, To Have Information To This Adoption:

Marion County Probate Court
Marion County Division of Family and Children

And then, my reply:

This letter is to hereby request ANY AND ALL INFORMATION regarding my birth, biological family and medical history. Enclosed is a copy of my driver's license and a copy of the letter sent to me by the Indiana State Department of Health.

The ISDH then sent what I had requested for most of my life. Although a photocopy, it was official and bore the embossed seal of Indiana. It was titled Certificate of Live Birth, and specified data that was always familiar to me. Under the large space given for the first, middle, and last name of father was center-spaced and typed *unknown*. At the bottom was the slanted signature of Dr. William Turner. There was another blank in which the doctor appeared to have made a mistake, blacking out the "yes" answer to Legitimate?___, and re-checked the box "no".

My last name was Price. The typed words dedicated to my first and middle name was not Jonathan Raymond, as my birth relatives mentioned, but was a single word -- "infant." Other than in her imagination, it seemed that Betty had never named me.

Despite turbulent adolescent years, I have felt blessed to live the life of an adoptee. When Betty was dismissed from Community Hospital on that cold February morning of 1958, she left without me. When she died, the reason for that decision died with her. However painful it was, I was thankful that she relinquished me. I was also thankful that Martha and Stoy Watson loved me enough to bear the responsibility of rearing me. I was disconcerted, however, that I had entered the world without an official name.

Enclosed with the copy of the birth certificate were three familiar papers. Yes, there they were again, staring me in the face; the Decree, the Petition for Custody of Child and the Order. I felt angry, knowing that the probate court had kept that information in a damp file folder for all those years. Glancing at one document again, I read something I didn't remember: "The court further finds that the prayer of said petitioners should be granted and that said adoption should be made and had as prayed for by the petitioners." There was never a prayer granted for Betty, however.

Another document I had never seen before was entitled, "Affidavit and Consent for Adoption", dated one day after my birth. The single page specified Betty Price as my natural mother, that she felt it was in my best interest to be adopted by Stoy and Martha Watson, and that she had made this decision on her own free will.

Then I saw Betty's signature. That was the first time I had ever seen her name written on the same form with my name and my parents, as if this mutual decision was made by everyone, including my one-day old self. And for a fleeting moment, I wondered what must have went through her mind when the pen was in her hand.

Although all evidence of Debra Kay has vanished other than her original birth certificate, I have shared the condensed petition I sent to the Superior Court in Kokomo, IN. If the reader happens to know of the whereabouts of my sister, please contact the author.

Dear Honorable Randy G. Hainlen,

This letter is to show good cause in my petition to open the sealed records of my sister, born as Debra Kay Price on December 6, 1955.

I am an adoptee. At seventeen years old I began the search for my birthmother.

On September 4, 1994, I met my Grandmother Hattie, Uncle Louie, Aunt Mary Jane, Uncle David, Aunt Joy Lee, and a first cousin. In 1995, I met my two brothers, Kenny Ray and Michael David. And on this Fourth of July weekend in Indianapolis, I met my sister, Suzie. Every member of our extended family has now united as one family.

Sadly, thirteen years prior to this first reunion, my birthmother passed away

Your Honor, Debra Kay is the last sibling to be reunited. If she is alive, she would never know that she has three brothers, one sister, and many relatives who want to meet her. I feel she has a right to witness that same joy of knowing her heritage. Although it was painful knowing that my birthmother died many years before our reunion, I can speak with experience that the joy of knowing how one originates in this world, having a past, and finding biological relatives and siblings far outweighs any pain.

Epilogue

A decade of wonderment has naturally instilled me with the ancient voyager's curiosity. Therefore, this book could never succinctly end. It is ironic that the conclusion of my journey has led me to the beginning of yet another -- the search for my sister, Debra Kay.

The only state record that seems to exist for Debra Kay is her birth certificate. There is no evidence that she was ever adopted in the state of Indiana, or that she was living in a foster home. Inharmonious with Betty's story, there was never a police or sheriff's report that she was kidnapped by a babysitter or social worker, or that she was even missing at all. The possibilities that seem to exist are that my sister was adopted in another state, given away, or God forbid, sold.

If she was subjected to the last two possibilities, I've been told many children have been given a "delayed certificate of birth", requested by the new parents. In the case of Debra Kay, she would be living in a surreal world, with a new name, birth date, and more unaware of her creation than I was.

But the portrait of that First Reunion continues to recount the joy we each shared on that wondrous day in September. I'm certain it will endure forever, and I hope it will give inspiration for those adoptees who want to know their roots. The picture currently rests on my desk at Gallery of Diamonds.

During the writing of this book, I witnessed the birth of my beautiful first child, Michaela. I even cut the umbilical cord. She will know her Mom and Dad. And, by reviewing the pages of her baby book, she will be able to discern her cosmic coordinates, and how she originated on this third planet from the sun.

But even to this day, when I am still in that semi-conscious state between reality and dreaming just before the alarm clock sounds, I sometimes catch myself calling out to Mom.

Martha Velia Watson. Born March 15, 1920. Author's adoptive mother at eighteen years old.

1947. Author's adoptive parents. Stoy Edward Watson. Born June 23, 1916. Died March 30, 1995, and Martha.

The author at fifteen months.

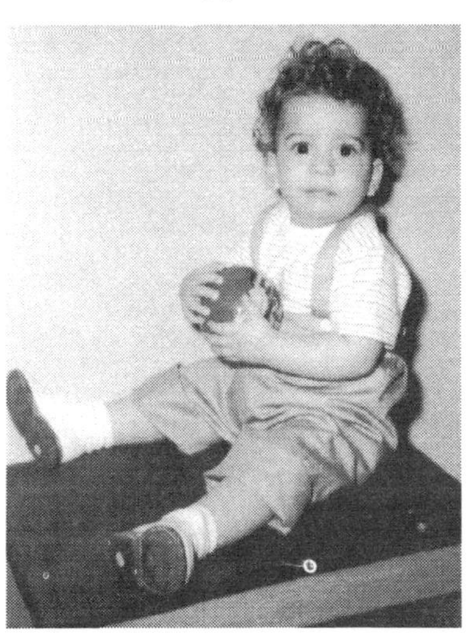

Primal beginnings. Author with adoptive mother. 1958.

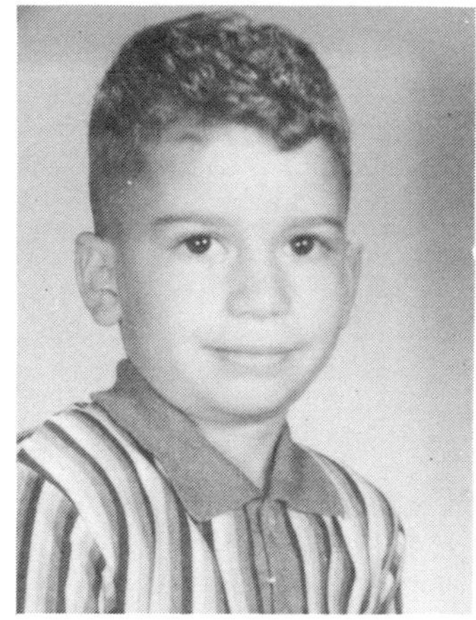

The search for physical similarity. First grade photos of birthmother, Betty Stewart, and the author. 1943 and 1965.

Betty (Stewart) Price and daughter, Debra Kay Price. Debra Kay was born December 6, 1955. Before her second birthday, she mysteriously disappeared. Readers please notify publisher with any information.

1957. Author's biological family in Coatesville, Indiana. L-R: Mother and brother, Betty and Michael David, Grandfather Otis Stewart, Aunt Mary Jane and Uncle Bob. Betty is shown pregnant with author.

1961. Betty with Michael David and Suzie.

Grandfather Otis Milton Stewart. Born April 13, 1899. Died May 14, 1987. Shown at eighteen years old.

Junior high photos of author and sister, Suzie, twenty years before either knew of the other's existence. The siblings met for the first time on July 5, 1996.

Biological grandparents Otis and Hattie Stewart. Fiftieth wedding anniversary, April 7, 1983.

Betty Gertrude Stewart. Born June 29, 1935. Died Steptember 19, 1981. Photo at age fourteen.

September 4, 1994. During this historic reunion, two families united as one. L-R, Uncle David and Joy Lee Stewart, Aunt Mary Jane and Louie Garland, cousin Michael Garland, Michael and Martha Watson, Grandmother Hattie Stewart and Stoy Watson. Photo by Carmen Watson.

Photos by Carmen Watson

1993. Out of 250 entries, sophomore Margaret Ketchersid from Huntington Beach, California was the very first diamond winner in the author's renown, "Why Mom Deserves a Diamond" essay contest. Mother, Ruth.

1994. Sophomore Alison Murphy from Mission Viejo, California was the diamond winner. Mother, Sandy.

1995. Chosen from over 2,000 essays, sixth-grade student Scott Kircher from Corona Del Mar, California was the diamond winner. Mother, Valerie.

1996. Seventh grade student Lauren Kiang, second from left, and fourth-grader Megan Darakjian were the diamond winners. Both are from Mission Viejo, Calfornia. Mothers, Kathleen and Lornna.

1997. L-R, Dianne Barraco and daughter, Jessica, Genevieve Slunka and mother, Sherry. Both from Irvine, Calfornia, Jessica and Genevieve were the diamond winners. $3,000 was presented to the Orange County Public Library from the sale of author's fifth anniversary anthology book.

Photos by Patricia Watson.

The fifth annual Mother's Day contest made history when 5,025 students submitted essays. Shown is the author and his wife, Carmen.

The Watson family: L-R, mother Martha Velia, Carmen, Michaela Maria, Adela Patricia and Michael.

Established in 1991, Gallery of Diamonds in Costa Mesa is now a major source for fine jewelry and diamonds in Southern California. The store has become renown for it's annual Mother's Day essay contest.

PART TWO
"Why Mom Deserves a Diamond" Essay Contest

Special Reading

In 1993, I heard of a jeweler who awarded a gemstone to a student who wrote the best Mother's Day essay. The notion of such an event excited me tremendously. I would sponsor a similar contest in recognition to my *two* Moms; the one who raised me and the one who gave birth to me. Although currently unsuccessful in finding the identity of my biological mother, I knew I would receive much satisfaction from encouraging young adults to express their appreciation for their own moms.

I announced to a few schools that I would award a one-quarter carat diamond to a student who wrote an essay which most creatively expressed, "Why Mom Deserves a Diamond." I coined the contest an academic exercise on motherly love.

I received two hundred and fifty entries from students who poured out their hearts, poetically illustrating why their moms should merit the gem. After reading each composition, I sorted them into two piles, then continued to evaluate them to the best of my ability, according to grade levels, sincerity, and writing talent. It was fascinating how each student expressed their appreciation for the woman who gave birth to them, and I could relate to most of their writings as if they were speaking about my own adoptive mother.

Reading each labor of love gave me a feeling of wholeness that was indescribable. With vibrant imagination, it was obvious that these young adults approached this voluntary writing assignment as a once-in-a-lifetime chance to honor their mothers. After I finished reading the last entry, I came to the realization that a never-before-discovered universal element: Mom, brought out the most creative expression of love, and that it was a common denominator of everyone's mind and heart.

After the most difficult task of designating a winner, I flipped through about a hundred other brilliant entries that were candidates for the grand prize. At that moment I felt it was unfair for only one individual out of two hundred and fifty to win. After reading those entries I selected fifty *second place* winners, choosing to award them garnets imported from Mozambique, Africa. Although less valuable than the grand prize, they were indeed beautiful and luscious gemstones and their captivating reddish color seemed symbolic for the occasion.

On that Sunday, Mother's Day, the winners were notified to come and receive their gemstone awards. Many mothers had no idea what their child had written until they came to the store, and it was heartwarming to see their elation.

Gallery of Diamonds then published an anthology booklet of the fifty-one winning entries entitled, "Why Mom Deserves a Diamond, In Remembrance of Mother's Day- 1993." If the students had rendered their gemstones to their mothers, they would still have a tangible reward for their achievement: a booklet that proudly displayed their winning composition.

What began as nothing more than a simple writing contest evolved into a movement in which students would be recognized for their creative achievements and at the same time become a little closer to their moms. Writers would be motivated to do their very best, and mothers of winners would receive a gem that would endure as a symbol of their child's appreciation.

The following spring, local high school students asked if we would be sponsoring another writing contest. The fervor of the second contest had begun. That year it was announced that not only would a diamond be awarded for the grand prize, but also ten sapphires for second place winners, and two hundred garnets for third place winners.

Entries invaded the store by the hundreds. Teachers would hand deliver heavy manilla folders with their entire English classes, sometimes winking at me and playfully remarking that the best ones were on top. Faxes would be spilled onto the floor. Parents would either personally submit their children's entries or slip them through the mail slot after hours. The mailman was constantly bewildered, wondering how a diamond business could suddenly receive daily basket loads of "jewelry orders."

Diamond Winners 1993-1997

Year	Winner	Grade	School	City
1997	Genevieve Slunka	11	Irvine High	Irvine, CA
1997	Jessica Barraco	4	Eastshore	Irvine, CA
1996	Megan Darakjian	4	Cordillera	Mission Viejo, CA
1996	Lauren Kiang	7	La Paz	Mission Viejo, CA
1995	Scott Kircher	6	Harbor Day	Corona del Mar, CA
1994	Alison Murphy	10	Capistrano Valley	Mission Viejo, CA
1993	Margaret Ketchersid	10	Edison	Huntington Beach,CA

By the deadline, the gentle hill of entries on my desk had erected itself into a mountain, for fourteen hundred and twenty-five poems and essays had been submitted. Once again, one submission moved me completely, and the reader may enjoy this first place composition in the following, *Past Diamond Winners.*

The 1994 contest marked the beginning of Gallery of Diamonds' event of the year, and although the store incessantly swarmed with students awaiting their gemstones, I believe I was fortunate enough to meet every single winner.

Although the quality of the gemstones were virtually the same, I offered each student the excitement of seizing his or her own colorful gem from the parcel with a pair of jewelers tweezers. They in turn would re-distribute the gem to their mothers. For the ten sapphire winners, the employees would acknowledge their accomplishment by applauding. Soon the entire store would reverberate with applause.

We published a second anthology booklet of the 1994 winners and donated the proceeds to the Orange County Public Library. It was a delightful feeling to be able to send that first check for seven hundred dollars, in which fifty-five copies of inspiring books were purchased for twenty of the county branches.

The 1995 contest garnered an amazing two thousand entries. The first place entry from a sixth-grade student was melodic, sincere, and came straight from the heart. This poem can also be enjoyed at the end of this section.

4,675 entries were submitted by our fourth year. This was the first year in which a diamond was awarded to two students. Both entries were outstanding for their grade levels. The highlight of that year was when both winners recited their essays live on the Orange County Newschannel. The essays are in *Past Diamond Winners*, and I know the reader will obtain as much enjoyment from them as I did.

By 1997, a staggering 5,025 essays were submitted for our fifth year anniversary contest. Stacked in a single vertical pile on a desk, they went halfway to the ceiling. Anticipating the response to that year's event, the maximum words were reduced to forty-five, for if it were greater I would surely still be reading them. A special thanks goes to my wife, Carmen, for her hours of opening and sorting the mail and for her miraculous ability of scheduling over one thousand families to come obtain their gemstone prizes.

At the time of publishing, the Gallery of Diamonds' "Why Mom Deserves a Diamond" writing contest has become a renown affair in Orange County, California, for its recognition of talented young authors. The contest has now spread to Los Angeles county, and future plans include other areas of the United States. The contest has been instrumental in giving kids an uplifting sense of pride, as proven by the many students who have started their own creative writing clubs.

Since this publication I have had the joy of reading every entry submitted, and I am exhilarated to have played a part in magnifying the goal of that one lone jeweler-- to award a gemstone to a brilliant student.

It is ironic that while reading thousands of essays on mom, I was also searching for the woman who gave birth to me. It is even more ironic that between the second and third contest I discovered the whereabouts of my birthmother. Sadly, she had died before I had a chance to meet her. I was thrilled, however, to have had several reunions with my *new* family.

			--No. of Gemstone Winners--		
Year	Entries	Max Words	Diamond	Sapphire	Garnet
1998	?	30	2	0	3,500
1997	5,025	40	2	25	975
1996	4,675	45	2	30	700
1995	2,016	70	1	40	350
1994	1,425	100	1	10	200
1993	250	100	1	0	50

The "Why Mom Deserves a Diamond" contest has become even more symbolic as an exercise on love, and I am quite sure the thought process involved for every writer instills a moral to appreciate one's own parents, whether adoptive or not, and *especially while they are living*. I hope the following most treasured essays will instill the same moral for the reader.

For those who desire to own any anthology book from the previous contest years, an order form is available at the end of this book.

Past Diamond Winners

1997

Burning sands, ever shifting
Desert of life I must pass through
When I sink, two hands are lifting
Helping me to start anew
She's the oasis where I may rest
She, who always knows me best
Diamond in the rough

Genevieve Slunka, Grade: 11
Irvine High School
Irvine, CA

My mom is a cozy place
Like a warm cup of cocoa
Or a pillow trimmed with lace
My Mom's love is all mine
I can always depend
She's more than a mom
She's my best friend

Jessica Barraco, Grade: 4
Eastshore Elementary
Irvine, CA

1996

Shadows flickering, dancing about
Even the moon is terrified
I lie wide awake, petrified as the distant
Silhouettes come dancing towards me
Then suddenly they disappear
As she flicks on the light
Her soothing smile, her comforting voice
And the monsters are all gone

Lauren Kiang, Grade: 7
La Paz Intermediate
Mission Viejo, CA

1996

A Mother Recipe

Million gallons of love, two pinches of creativity, twelve cups of niceness, two gallons of understanding. Million drops of unique and beautifulness, any other items that might make your mother wonderful.

Mix well, bake two seconds.
I guarantee a mother!

Megan Ashley Darakjian, Grade: 4
Cordillera
Mission Viejo, CA

1995

Whether I stand on land or shore
I know I couldn't love my mother more
Driving me to the homes of friends
Her cheerfulness never ends
Always caring, always there
In times that are good
In times of despair
Magical lands we like to explore
When she reads aloud
From classical lore
I thank you, Mom, at each day's end
You really are my best friend

Scott Kircher, Grade: 6
Harbor Day School
Corona del Mar, CA

In Search Of Mom

1994

No one knows what it's like
To walk in her shoes
When every game she played with me
She always seemed to lose

And the note from Santa Claus
Seemed to look the same
As the writing on the lunchbags
Where she wrote my name

In all the falls I took
And the cuts I made
She fixed me up with only a
Kiss and a purple band-aid

With all the things I didn't do
And all the things she knew
I'd never thought I'd see the day
I saw us moving further away

But of all the things she ever said
And all the nights sleeping in my bed
I promised I'd give her
The diamonds in the sky
When all she said she ever wanted
Were the diamonds in my eyes

Alison Murphy, Grade 10
Capistrano Valley High School
Mission Viejo, CA

1993

Her love is not blind
It is clear and forgiving
Her touch is all-knowing
Her joy is life giving
This angel, my mother, gives of herself
And illuminates me
With compassion's true wealth

A symbol of courage
And strength she remains
And understands all my joys and pains
To gaze at my mother
Who strives beyond duty
Is to see radiate
Her unique warming beauty!
The sweet voice of mother
Her strong, safe, embrace
I long to possess
Her pure, natural, grace
My Mother, my guide
And gemstone so rare
Deserves out of likeness
A diamond as fair

Margaret Ketchersid, Grade 10
Edison High School
Huntington Beach, CA

Outstanding Mother's Day Essay Winners from the Past

Alderwood Basics Plus

Irvine, CA

Everything she does is
special in a grand way
Everything she says
inspires me every day
Her special touch
makes me feel wonderful
She handles things
in a manner so peaceful
No artist can capture her essence
I smile at her presence

Sheena Ghanbari
Grade: 6
1996 winner

Brighter than stars
More valuable than gold
Sweeter than honey
Yet stands alone

Planting happiness
Sowing love
Mom stands
From all up above

A gift from God
To the Gardener of Love
A diamond glistens
As it descends from above

To Mom, a diamond...

Tammy Huang
Grade: 6
1996 sapphire winner

Aliso Elementary

Lake Forest, CA

Here I sit in the branches of this evergreen trying to compare you to everything I see. Your giving heart is the outstretched arms of the branches. Your courage the small plants below struggling for life. Your creativity the different design of every flower.

Lauren Marie Bielefeld
Grade: 6
1996 sapphire winner

Aliso Viejo Middle

Aliso Viejo, CA

Love is the vitalizing, nourishing, sustaining electricity of life. I am electrified because of my mother. She loves me unconditionally and I have found no flaws in her expression of love. Her smile has a balanced symmetry, and her pleasant karma is dispersed throughout her family...

I am thankful to be blessed with such a warmhearted mother. I believe she, the most valuable and genuine person I know, deserves the most brilliant of all gems.

Brandi Andrews
Grade: 8
1994 winner

My Mom: A Diamond Within Herself

Her hair as dark as the fathoms below
That must be why I love her so
Her smile's so bright
It shines like the North star's light

Her eyes sparkle like
diamonds in the sky
Her lips are like rubies that I spy
When she enters a room
my excitement grows
My happiness greatly shows
Never a sad face, never a tear
In my heart she's always near
Perfect in every way
Our love increases night and day
Never worried by poorness
or with wealth
She is a diamond within herself

Nakisa Aschtiani
Grade: 8
1994 sapphire Winner

My mommy has
The beauty of a diamond
Yet she isn't vain
Her personality shines with laughter
And she sprinkles joy over pain
She is the sweetest of art
She is the priceless diamond I wear
in my heart

Sarah Demers
Grade: 7
1997 sapphire winner

Anaheim High School

Anaheim, CA

She brought life into the world,
Cradles in her arms,
She vowed never to have the child
To be engulfed by the treacherous
whirlwinds of life.
Fears turned into hopes
Dreams became visions of reality.
In the midst of the darkness
She is my beam of light.
Her love abounds with no limits--
Like a diamond that can
never be crushed.
She is my mother.
And never can I recompense
For all her sacrifices
That she has made for me.
And for that I am forever grateful.
A diamond is forever
Like my love for her!

Thuy Tran
Grade: 11
1993 winner

Ball Junior High

Anaheim, CA

My mother is not always the perfect mother who sews my clothes, bakes me cookies or has the bed made when I come home from school. Although she always knows where I am, cares about my feelings, and makes sure I have a safe secure and loving home to call my own. My mother has always encouraged me to express myself, to make my own decisions, and to fight for what I believe is right. If I could give a gift to the world I would make sure every child has a mother like mine.

Leah Hollenbeck
Grade: 7
1994 sapphire winner

Bonita Canyon

Irvine, CA

My mother is like a flower flowing in the wind. In the middle of the flower is a bright dazzling diamond. The diamond brings out the caring, loving look in her eyes. When she sways back and forth her beautiful fragrance fills the air. Her colorful petals bloom. She then cares for her seedlings through the deepness of her heart. She loves her family and shall always be with them.

Cory Morrow
Grade: 5
1995 sapphire winner

Brea Country Hills

Brea, CA

Mother
Whenever I hear this gentle word
I think of someone who cares for me
Mother
Her eyes are twinkling, cheerful, and bright
With golden hair like the rising sun
Mother
She's always wearing a joyful smile
Her love will continue forever
Mother

Kendra Dix
Grade: 6
1996 winner

My mom is a diamond in the rough. She always puts herself behind everyone and everything. My mom never asks for anything in return for her love and generosity. I feel my mom deserves a diamond because she sparkles with honesty, love and devotion.

Jennifer Sutton
Grade: 5
1996 sapphire Winner

California Elementary

Costa Mesa, CA

Lots of kids have great mothers, but I think my mother deserves a diamond because she's extra wonderful. She teaches me to be more independent and coaches me on my swimming, piano, school, and tap dance. Plus it's awesome to have a microbiologist as your mother! It' so interesting to see those icky fungi under a microscope and to learn about diseases in the body! I sure love my mother!

Laura Wong
Grade: 4
1995 winner

Calvary Christian

Santa Ana, CA

Diamonds are a woman's best friend. My mother is my best friend, as well as a mentor and advocate to me. If my mom had one precious stone for everything she did for me, there wouldn't be enough diamonds, nor any other jewels.

I can always count on her to be there for me. I love her immensely, and humbly dedicate this silent message of love to her.

Falon Bahal
Grade: 7
1995 sapphire winner

Diamonds resemble perfection. My mother is like a diamond to me. They are both almost flawless. Diamonds are a girl's best friend, as my mother is to me. They are beautiful, amazing, and outstanding, inside and out! One of the greatest gifts she could receive is a diamond. Her love and sacrifice is worth a gem!

Laurie Myers
Grade: 8
1995 winner

My mom deserves a diamond because she has devoted her time to polishing her children's many facets, throughout life, in trying to make us as flawless as perfect diamonds.

She herself is like a rare gem that stands out like a diamond in the rough. She is unlike a manmade diamonique but made by God especially for her children and sent from heaven to be a sparkle in our lives.

Katie Woodall
Grade: 8
1995 sapphire winner

Capistrano Valley

Mission Viejo, CA

From fathoms below
white caps o' the sea
Among the luminescent creatures
To the dizzying heights of ranges, there
One of the world's greatest treasures

The trustworthy advice
of the babbling brook
The inviting paddies of spanish moss
For these I love my mom

Jean Kanjanavaikoon
Grade: 10
1996 winner

A counselor, friend,
chauffeur and nurse
Knowing what's right or wrong
What is better, what's worse
That's who my mother is

All she wants is the happiness of my sister and I
She tells us we put
the sparkle in her eye
That's who my mother is

Because she's done so much
With hardly a huff or puff
Because I haven't done nearly enough
That's why she deserves a diamond

Tina Basu
Grade: 9
1995 sapphire winner

A Star For All To See

A woman of many,
challenged every turn
Yet always succeeding,
with her love still a-burn
Plagued by Lupus, disease of wolves
Which often flails at her,
but she proves it of fools
Taking what she learns,
through courage and pain
She turns it into love,
honesty, and no shame
She cries a single tear,
and taken from her face
She gives us this diamond star,
for all the human race

Jason Daniel Thompson
Grade: 11
1995 sapphire winner

Carden School

Fountain Valley, CA

I was adopted by my mom
She loves me more than her cat, Tom
We have a lot between us two
When she smiled our love grew
Before I was adopted I felt lonely
Now I feel better and I am treated nicely

Julianna Reanee Notti
Grade: 5
1996 winner

Century High School

Santa Ana, CA

Nine long inseparable months
She carried me within her
She fed me over five years
With her own milk

For three hungry years
She risked her life for mine
She became a thief just to feed
My tiny stomach
Once she was caught and almost

executed for her crime
She risked her life to escape
So I would not grow up without a mother
Khmer Rouge, you disgusting animals for
The hardship you put my mother through

No one and no thing
Can replace her
Because she is my mother--
My living stream

Steve Lee
Grade: 12
1994 winner

No nobler thought my soul may claim
No softer word my tongue may frame
Of all the compassion,
sweetness and love
Of all the goodness of heaven
Above God bless my dear mother
To one who bears the sweetest name
And adds a luster to the same
Who shares my joy
Cheers me up when I am sad
The greatest friend I've ever had
Long life to her, for there's no other
Who takes the place of my dear mother

Deborah Perez
Grade: 11
1994 sapphire winner

Corona del Mar High

Newport Beach, CA

As hard as a diamond in the inside
As pretty as one from a distance
She glitters and shines
as a light hitting a facet.

Her grace and beauty is hard to compare
To the years it takes to make a diamond.

My mother is kind and gentle as a
precious rock
Wouldn't hurt a fly and
These are her rules etched in stone
She loves the world with all her heart
And the last wish she has
Is to have a stone and me by her side
For she loves us both.

Robert Hacker
Grade: 7
1993 winner

Mother, a word used by many and used by me. Yet my mother is much more, she is a mentor, a dreamer, and an inventor. My mother is a teacher and teachers make people learn. My mother is like a bird. Kind and loving like a dove, wise and skillful as an owl, and as determined as an eagle to stay alive in a dying world. My mother deserves a diamond to put the sparkle back in her eyes and so people know she tries.

Robert Shenk
Grade: 7
1993 winner

A diamond for my mother?
Why, that is absurd!
My mother deserves a platinum ring
And all the riches that I've heard
For all the times she's been there
For all the times she's cared
For all the times and facts of life
That she has always shared

She doesn't let me date, yet
I've been grounded once or twice
And before my dying day,
I'll have been scolded more than thrice

My mom deserves a diamond?
Well, please excuse me, sir,
But unless it is the Cullinan
It's not good enough for her

Rebecca Whitney Wright
Grade: 7
1993 winner

Costa Mesa High School

Costa Mesa, CA

While I would die, that she might live,
She has given me everything
she has to give.
Giving of herself, she seeks
nothing in return;
I talk to her daily, from her past, I learn.
When she says she loves me, I know
it's sincere;
There's a place in my heart where I hold
her dear.
God gave her to me, she's like no other
I'd just like to tell her... "I love you
mother!"

Tawney Bayes
Grade: 9
1993 winner

Currie Middle School

Tustin, CA

What is a mother?
Is a mother a person
who wipes away your tears
Or does she chase away
your darkest fears?
She works so hard, she cares so much
Your worries melt away
at her single touch
But through the years she was there
To help brush your teeth
and comb your hair
From when you took your very first step
To when you married, then she wept
It's when she's lost her baby,
And her smile's gone
You realize you love her enough
To call her mom

Michelle Ryan
Grade: 7
1995 sapphire winner

Del Cerro

Mission Viejo, CA

My mom's sparkling eyes glimmer and shimmer like a diamond. Her smooth hair is like the surface of a diamond. Her enchanting words and gentle hands soothe and guide me when I'm nervous or intense. Such a good-hearted mom should truly deserve a diamond.

Tina Toosky
Grade: 5
1996 sapphire winner

Dwyer Middle School

Huntington Beach, CA

No poem can tell how much I love you
No story can explain how great you are
No words can say
all the good you've done
Believe me, I've tried!

You're the best mom around
Compared to all my friends
The prettiest one, too
You deserve the diamond the most
Believe me, I know!

You deserve the diamond the most
Because you're loved the most
Believe me, you are!

Lindsey Speegle
Grade: 6
1995 sapphire winner

God made a wonderful mother
A mother who never grows old
In her eyes He placed
bright shining stars
In her cheeks, fair roses, you see
God made a wonderful mother

And gave that dear mother to me

Briana Haft
Grade: 7
1997 sapphire winner

Strawberry blonde hair
Sparkling blue and green eyes
These are characteristics about my mom
That I really prize

She devoted her life to me
When I was a very young juvenile
She was a single, hardworking mother
Who always found time to smile

My mother is a special friend
That I could always depend on
To help me and comfort me
When something goes wrong

Nicholas Hangca
Grade: 6
1995 sapphire winner

I know my mom would love a jewel
But that's against my golden rule
My mother shall never wear a stone
She looks too pretty on her own
Her silky hair and porcelain skin
Would make the gem look like a sin
Her pearly teeth and dancing eyes
Don't need further to beautify
My mother is a precious thing
For her I would do anything
Including earning a diamond ring

Chelsea Lindman
Grade: 6
1995 sapphire winner

Eastshore Elementary

Irvine, CA

I think my mom deserves a diamond because she's there for me whenever I need her. She cooks great, she cleans great. Plus the time that we had enough money to pay for a diamond ring, we bought one for my grandma.

Another reason I feel she deserves one is that she's very outgoing, smart, artistic, and loving. And most of all she's just a great SuperMom!

Stacey McClurg
Grade: 5
1994 sapphire winner

My Mom is just the best!
She's better than the rest
She helps me with my tasks
And answers what I ask
She reads to me at night
And sends my dreams aflight
She's upbeat and will say
"Make the most of each day
Life's for living- give it a try
Always have hope and ne'er day die."

Jimmy Pollard
Grade: 4
1995 sapphire winner

Edison High School

Huntington Beach, CA

You took away my broken dreams
And spliced them to repair
Made me into a teen
Whose thoughts ran wild
And encouraged me to care
Not locked away forever
But displayed for all to see
To see that glimmer
Which depicts your light in me

Logan Saito
Grade: 10
1996 sapphire winner

SHE IS MOTHER

A shape of a woman
with the figure of Eve.
A woman with the strength of stone.
The softness of a woman of grace.
An innocent, intelligent face.

She touches every soul.
She shines like diamonds and pearls.
She is the ultimate woman.
She is Mother.

Yana Yanovsky
Grade: 12
1993 winner

Since the day I was born my mother has been there. She's walked beside me, held my hand, and showed me how much she cares. She brought me through my toughest times.
On her I can depend.
From now until eternity.
She'll be my best friend.

Karin Coulter
Grade: 10
1996 winner

Beautiful, precious, and elegant. Practical, strong, and pure. Not only do these qualities describe a diamond, but they also portray my mother. As a child she was my protector, now my confider. My mother deserves a diamond because she is one.

Amanda Lam
Grade: 10
1996 winner

My mom is one of my best friends. Her unfailing love and support for me is overwhelmingly amazing. She always takes time out to explore the wonders of life with me. It is truly impossible to measure her infinite perfections.

Emma Parker
Grade: 10
1996 winner

A crowd is flocking
to Gallery of Diamonds
Money and checkbooks in hand
My mother gives me
a warm, gentle smile
And looks at her own wedding band
She has taught me always that
happiness comes
Not from the riches we own
The love and warmth of a family is all
That we need to feel at home

My mother deserves
the best things in life
For she works much more
than she should
But to me she already
sparkles much more
Than a diamond ever could

Jennifer Field
Grade: 10
1994 sapphire winner

Ocean breeze warm and calm
Loving touch never gone
Strong and willing, always giving
My love for her will never fade
Open minded, optimistic
Her mind is always clear
This woman is so special
She's my mother who is dear

Meghan Watson
Grade: 11
1997 sapphire winner

El Camino Real

Irvine, CA

Mother- the pearl inside an oyster
The joys of my day
The cream inside an oreo
And the flowers in May

The prize within a box of crackerjacks
The rainbow after a storm
The center of an artichoke
And the love that keeps you warm

Judy Tran
Grade: 6
1996 sapphire winner

El Modena High

Orange, CA

For all the times she let me hide
For all the tears she ever dried
For all the times she knew I lied
Mom deserves a diamond

For every smile she has given me
For every fault she's helped me see
For every person she's let me be
Mom deserves a diamond

For all the inches I have grown
For all the trust I have ever known
For all the love she has ever shown
Mom deserves a diamond

Sinda Osburn
Grade: 11
1994 sapphire winner

Ensign School

Newport Beach, CA

5...4...3...2...1... My mom was forever changed in five seconds. Life dealt her a nasty blow when she got in a car accident. She was left walking on a cane for life. My family had just come out of a poor period when my mom used to starve herself so my sister and I could eat. She battled for our custody twice. She always gave us our best. Even though we were poor, we didn't know it. She is strict because she wants what's best for me. For this and more my mother deserves a diamond for all she has given me unconditionally.

Jeremy LaMantia
Grade: 7
1994 winner

Fairmont Private

Anaheim, Ca

If I pick a flower I think of my mother. She is a rose and I am the stem. I love the ways she reads to me. She's as sweet as a daisy. I love her very much like bees love honey.

Andrea Quant
Grade: 2
1996 winner

Fountain Valley High

Fountain Valley, CA

Like a diamond,
my Mom is a radiant light.
Her love and friendship make
everything bright!
She is kind, generous, and
compassionate, too.
She supports me in all that I do!

Like a diamond,
my Mom is genuine and true.
Her loving qualities
always shine through!
My Mom is a person in whom I confide.
This precious jewel is
always by my side!

Like a diamond,
she is a lasting treasure.
The depth of her love
is without measure!
My Mom deserves a diamond
for what she is to me.
She's the inspiration for all I strive to be!

Tricia Michels
Grade: 9
1993 winner

Hankey, Carl Elementary

Mission Viejo, Ca

My Mom has a smile that SHINES! We are "roomies" in life. Always a smile for me and others. "Have faith and a good heart" is what Mom taught me. I am proud of her inner beauty.

I love you Mom- my guiding light.

Kaprice Vargas
Grade: 3
1996 sapphire winner

Harbor Day

Corona del Mar, Ca

A delicate rose in a patch of weeds
A glass star in a handful of beads
A gleaming jewel in a mine of coal
A spark of light in a dark, black hole
A person seeming always calm
Could be no one but my mom

Tina Codini
Grade: 7
1996 sapphire winner

You are a shining light among a world of darkness, guiding me through tough times. You are tender, sincere, caring and kind. Through your wise words, you have taught me right from wrong. You are my heart and soul, and I love you.

Ashley Jacobson
Grade: 8
1996 winner

Harbor View

Corona del Mar, CA

My mom deserves a diamond
Because she does her best
She helps me and she cleans the house
With barely time to rest
She takes me places and I'm never late
She's always kind with a great fate
Whenever I'm with her
she's always caring
Sometimes she can also be daring
She's very responsible everyday
If I'm ever bored she'll even play
That's why my mom deserves a diamond

Lauren Grumet
Grade: 5
1995 sapphire winner

Hayden Elementary

Westminster, CA

One who can bear no more
Just needs a simple task or chore
Far or near. She loves me dear
To the end she's my best friend
She is smart. A piece of art, from God's heart. There's only one.
And that's my mom.

Angela. C. Mendez
Grade: 3
1996 sapphire winner

Irvine High

Irvine, CA

A diamond and my mother
Are two of the same
Diamonds all around her
Sparkles in her name

For never has there been
A dark and starless night
For with the shining
of my mother's eyes
From darkness comes light

Dew on morning rose,
diamonds in the sky
Kind words when a new day starts
All these things I see in her--
The diamond of my heart

Lauren M. O'Hara
Grade: 9
1995 sapphire winner

My mother sailed alone into a land of glass walls

Walls of traffic and children
Calling elders by last names
But my mother has a diamond
Of old ways from China
And with this immigrant's tool
She slices America's glass
And reaches her arms through

Michael Tan
Grade: 11
1996 winner

La Paz Intermediate

Mission Viejo, CA

Simple, mild, unnoticed. I'm my mother's wall. She is my stencil. When she touches me, I feel warm. From start to finish, she has a loving stroke. As she paints my life, she watches her greatest work mature into adulthood.

Joslin Beck
Grade: 7
1997 sapphire winner

To the one I love

A sparkling smile, cherry red lips
Light rosy cheeks and soft finger tips
A passionate heart burns with love
And beautiful things that she dreams of
A soothing voice, a warm embrace
Brings a smile upon my face...
Mom

Stefanie Jednoralski
Grade: 7
1996 sapphire winner

My mom is my diamond
Priceless you see
Nobody demonstrates
Less flaws than she
Shows me her love
In every way
Does many favors
For me everyday
Helps me to sparkle
Helps me to laugh
Inspires me to speak
These words on her behalf

Cindy Mescher
Grade: 7
1996 sapphire winner

Da Vinci shaped the Mona Lisa, Van Gogh sketched the Starry Night. Shaping what is to come, like classics done before, my mother is sculpting my life. She is depicting the way.

Eric Reed
Grade: 7
1997 sapphire winner

Loara High

Anaheim, CA

I thank you mom, for this day of life. For feet to walk amidst the trees. For hands to pick the flowers from the earth. For a sense of smell to breath in the sweet perfumes of nature. For a mind to think about the magic of everyday miracles and appreciate your tender love and care. Thanks to you and God for your Guidance. I love you mom.

Maricela Rubalcava
Grade: 12
1996 winner

Los Naranjos

Irvine, CA

My mother deserves a diamond because she is the mother of the world. When I have a cut, she will heal it for me. When I have something on my mind, she will talk to me about it. When I am feeling sad, she will cheer me up. When I have to cry, her shoulder is right beside me.

I love my mother very much.
I am very lucky.

Natalie Maatouck
Grade: 5
1995 sapphire winner

Mariners

Newport Beach, CA

As my mother opened the green velvety box, I saw the color drain from her face and little drops of water rolled down her face. As she held the stunning diamond up, the sunlight reflected off of it and colored the room the color of the rainbow. "Honey", she said."It's gorgeous!"

My mom deserves a diamond because I want her to know how special she is to me.

Ayesha Gasdorf
Grade: 5
1995 sapphire winner

Mater Dei High

Santa Ana, CA

A delicate rosebud on a thorny bush
Soak up the water, so generously given
Open to the sunlight
Radiating down just for you
Spread out in the soil,
carefully tendered
And blossom forth one day
With the love showered upon you

Christina Irving
Grade: 9
1996 winner

Mission Parish School

San Juan Capistrano, CA

It would be silly to question
Why Mom deserves the prize
Anyone can say that
She is always so wise
She is kind and gentle
Mom rarely has a fit
Mom cares for me
Mom loves me
Mom knows when I need help

Through sickness and health
Mom has been by my side
And those are the reasons
Mom deserves the prize

Jane Donahue
Grade: 4
1995 sapphire winner

Mommy is the core of my apple, the fluff in my pillow, the heat for my popcorn, and the bird making my nest. Mommy is the center of my life. My supporter. My inspiration. And the building block for my future.

Jennifer Kissee
Grade: 7
1997 sapphire winner

My mother deserves a diamond because they have so much in common. During the day, she's sparkly and bright. But at night she's calm and quiet-- just like a diamond.

There is one thing they don't have in common! A diamond might get old or break. But my love for my mother never will.

Amy Monin
Grade: 5
1995 sapphire winner

Mother is like a garden. Her lips are bright like a red rose. Her brown eyes sparkle like butterflies in sunshine. Her skin reminds me of peaches. Her voice like that of the birds. I see her everywhere around me.

Cristy Robinson
Grade: 4
1997 sapphire winner

Moulton

Laguna Niguel, CA

She loves me so dearly
I love her so clearly
I think she is the sweetest person to live
Maybe on Earth, Saturn, Jupiter, Mars
I look in her eyes, I see the stars
So please give my mom the diamond

Danny Peart
Grade: 4
1996 winner

Paularino

Costa Mesa, CA

A comforting hug, a warm smile
Twinkling eyes, her hair in a neat pile
Humorous jokes, her beautiful voice
Soft skin, her laugh makes us rejoice
Her luscious lips, her loving look
Inviting hands, and what a good cook!

Katy Renish
Grade: 6
1997 sapphire winner

Perry Elementary

Huntington Beach, CA

Minute Maid Premium:
She is always ready to help at a MINUTES notice; Whether it be for a JUICY time or a DELICIOUS event. She is a 100% PURE love with a CONCENTRATED heart. ORIGINAL MINUTE MOM.

Amanda Bautista
Grade: 5
1997 sapphire winner

Portola Middle School

Orange, CA

A diamond is forever. So is a mother. But a mother is more precious. A mother is the one thing that stays forever imprinted in your heart and mind.

My mother is the best thing that ever happened to me. She is the sole reason I came into being and I love her. Without her I would be nothing. She stands always by my side. She guards me with her life, shielding me in all her weakness. She will be with me forever in mind and soul, and a place for her will always remain in my heart.

Melissa Vadnais
Grade: 8
1994 winner

Prince of Peace

Orange, CA

My mom is awesome
She is as pretty as a blossom
I care about her so much
She just has a magic touch
I can't explain it but
She is the best mom in the world
She is so keen
Do you know what I mean?
So that is why I think
She should get the diamond thing

Ryan Underwood
Grade: 4
1995 sapphire winner

Rancho San Joachin

Irvine, CA

To Be A Mother
A mother's duty never ends
Her strength will never grow weary
A mother's care she always sends
A mother's hope is never dreary

In Search Of Mom

Mo'erhood is a lifelong career
Her laughter fills the darkest space
Even from afar her thoughts are near
Her ever open arms embrace

No greater love exists in life
Life's lessons she wisely teaches
She hears of troubles and of strife
And her loving warmth outreaches

Elaine Auyoung
Grade: 8
1995 sapphire winner

She does much more than dry my tears
She does much more
than quell my fears
She starts the fire in my mind
Reveals my soul for me to find
Inspires me to reach the sky
Gives me strength enough to fly
But more than that,
she's true, she's real
A spirit who hurts and laughs and feels
Her effort is touching
and funny and sweet
She'll try till she's sore
From her head to her feet
No, my mother doesn't need carats
To make her soul shine
But I think a diamond would be just fine

Ellen Chen
Grade: 8
1995 sapphire winner

Undisguised in pride, eyes shine
A gleam of incandescent light
Welling heart grows warm unguarded
What reason does the soul glow bright?
Tender glance with softened eyes
Concerns for warmth
and comfort, strong
For her own cares she worries not
For whom she sings a soothing song?
More valuable than finest treasure
Mother's care is valued high
Her family her heart's sole delight
A glance and then a loving sigh

Kristen Lara
Grade: 8
1995 sapphire winner

Her understanding surrounds me
like gentle waves
Roads of comfort,
with her love she paves
In the heart that loves her

She could have been a rose,
bright ruby red
Or a pearl, for tears of happiness shed
And tears she has wiped
from a tender young face
And filled up with love
a once empty space
In the heart that loves her

Many names in
many languages has she
But she shall always be "Mom" to me
The heart that loves her

Lauren Lavoie
Grade: 7
1994 sapphire winner

Just as I abandon all hope
Each and every time she comes
No one brightens my day like her
Nothing close to taking her place
In the day, during nights
Forever there to help me grow
Even if I don't always appreciate
Resting not a second

Listening to my problems
Is my mother, patiently waiting
Until I finish, to give a solution

(Editors note: This is an acrostic. The first letter of each line spells the name of the author's mother.)

Dennis Liu
Grade: 8
1995 sapphire winner

Mom deserves a diamond because, like a diamond, she's of the highest quality. Though a hard-working and busy single parent, mom always sacrifices her time and pleasures for me. I'd like her to know how much I love her. Of all the material objects that I could give to her, a diamond would be the most appropriate because, like the bonds between a mother and son, a diamond is forever.

Jonathan McIntye
Grade: 8
1995 sapphire winner

My first teacher
My first friend
You always love me, share with me
And are concerned about me
I always trust you, love you, and
respect you
Even when I grow up!
Even if I may become a doctor,
a lawyer...
I will never forget you
The wonderful mom I have
You are always the best in my heart
And you are the one
that deserves a diamond

Tony Qu
Grade: 7
1995 sapphire winner

Sowers

Huntington Beach, CA

You see a star sparkling
in the dark blue night
Each second it comes closer
Then falls in your outstretched arms
like a snowflake falling from a cloud,
But as you look closer
You see that this
beautiful sight is a diamond
shining in the pale moonlight
You bring the diamond to your heart
and begin on your way home
You go to your mother and say,
"One beautiful thing deserves another,"
and give her a kiss and continue
"For both came from heaven."
As you leave the room,
you get a glimpse
of a tear from her eye
Because she knows you love her
And today is Mother's Day.

Seth Braithwaite
Grade: 7
1994 winner

Her hair a golden color like the band
Her eyes sparkle like the jewel
Her words so soft, like tender love
That warms inside of you
Her mind as big as the whole world
Her ears so open wide
To listen to my every word
As she sits by my side
Her skin so soft and white as snow
She works so hard for me
I love her just so dearly because
God made her just for me!

Amanda Paugh
Grade: 7
1994 winner

Love is the word that enters my mind
Whether she's beside me
Or a shadow from behind
Holding me strong
with a caring loving bond
Always there to guide me
A star that shines upon dawn
My heart is filled with
mem'ries...thoughts of more to come
Through all the times and
tears we shared
Never once has our love
missed being bared
Her welcoming arms
Seem to take hold of me gently
As I sit looking
in those warm caring eyes
If all I had was a vision of my mother

Surely, it would be a diamond
That and none other

Dominique Hilsabeck
Grade: 7
1995 sapphire winner

St. Anne

Laguna Niguel, CA

My mom is a jewel
She glistens in the night
Like a diamond in the sky
Whenever I am sad
Her light makes me bright
I'm glad she's my mom
She's a diamond
Shining bright in my heart

Matt Walden
Grade: 5
1996 sapphire winner

St. Catherine

Laguna Beach, CA

For the endearing pain
That seizes her heart when I'm lost
For the tender cheek,
the cool, soft hands
That are available without any cost
For the softness smile,
the warmest heart
The gentleness of care
My mother deserves a diamond
Because she is always there

Kristen Adams
Grade: 8
1996 sapphire winner

St. Columban

Garden Grove, CA

She spreads her sunshine everywhere
With all the love she has to share
Her helping hand is always there
She knows I love her, I'm aware

I love my mom with all my heart
She was always there from the start
She's my best friend

Cassie Huger
Grade: 6
1996 winner

St. John the Baptist

Costa Mesa, CA

God gave me a gift that I love everyday
She is special to me in every way
She's someone who'll kiss an
Ouchy on your arm
She makes the hurt go away
With her special charm
She's like a guardian angel
Except my mom I can see
She's my mom
And she's special to me
So for her love and kindness
I would like to say
I love you mom and
Have a Happy Mother's Day!

Nicole Esquer
Grade: 6
1995 sapphire winner

St. Julianna

Fullerton, CA

Continual patience, kindness
And gentle hand is the start
Then follows her friendliness
Outgoing personality and loving heart
She's there for me night and day
Her wisdom and advice guide my way
This unique friend, like no other
Is the one I call "Mother"

Katie Spoorman
Grade: 8
1996 sapphire winner

Tewinkle

Costa Mesa, CA

My mother's personality is like a gem
She shines on the outside
But the value is within

Her hair is veins of gold
She cared for me
every time I had a cold
Her eyes have an iris of pure jade
She comforted me in the night
When I was afraid

When you look for her imperfections
You'll find close to none
Because my mother's love
Is as strong as a diamond

Shaun Brown
Grade: 8
1995 sapphire winner

Turtle Rock

Irvine, CA

The gentle touch.... melting away all silhouettes of evil. The wild spirit....standing strong. The generous heart....forever giving love and compassion. In her eyes, I see my past, my future. I see hope in the depths of her soul....

Emily Liu
Grade: 6
1997 sapphire winner

A heart of gold shining diamond eyes, My hand she holds, singing lullabies, whispering. Silvery raindrops of calmness glimmering in her serene face. Her radiant smile filled with warmness-- a reflection of love and of grace.

Emily Looney
Grade: 6
1997 sapphire winner

Valley High

Santa Ana, CA

My mom, the skilled seamstress
Is sewing the quilt of life
She does not know how it will turn out
But is certain it will be all right
Mending problems best as she can
Sewing the most important and
Necessary piece in the quilt...me!

Rocio Rosales
Grade: 10
1996 winner

Westwood Basics Plus

Irvine, CA

My mom is a special person
She hugs me and loves me all the time
She helps me do a lot of things
I might be scared to try
She takes me to the movies
The bookstore and the zoo
Mom, I'm really lucky to have you.

Ashlee Emmert
Grade: 3
1996 sapphire winner

I believe my mother is worthy of this diamond for she is a diamond herself. She sparkles when the light hits her and even when it doesn't, she is a diamond that will never chip but always keep on shining for years to come as she's shined on me for the last 10 years.

Tiffani Lynch
Grade: 5
1996 sapphire winner

Illness or parties,
my mom can handle anything

Loves me, and makes memories
Occasionally makes my favorite dinners

In Search Of Mom

Very good about
keeping the family running
Everyday she goes to work and helps
sick people

My mom donates clothes and
things to charity
Yells sometimes

My mom feeds me healthy foods
Occasionally we go to the mall
My mom is the best mom in the world!

(Editor's note. This author has written a secret message from the first letter of each line.)

Lindsey Marino
Grade: 5
1995 sapphire winner

Whitaker

Buena Park, CA

My mom deserves a diamond
For everything she has done for me
She saved me when I was in trouble
She was my strength when I was weak
I will always cherish her
And when she grows old, I'll help her
For everything she has done for me
My mom deserves a diamond

Rose Avramescu
Grade: 5
1996 winner

Used by permission, a few quotes about the "Why Mom Deserves a Diamond" essay contest are listed.

Thank you for giving my eighth graders the privilege of participating in your contest. Before writing, we had a heartwarming discussion on "Mother" -- what she means to me, how I value her, and what life would be without her. I wish it were on tape. For sure, some eyes were opened." Joan Collignon. Rancho San Joaquin Middle School. Irvine. CA.

"Thank you for promoting motherly love and communicating this idea through writing." Patti Tromberg. Vista View School. Fountain Valley, CA.

"This could be the Mother of all Mother's Day contests!" Theresa Walker. The Orange County Register.

"His long-time search for his birthmother has made this jeweler especially sensitive to the significance of Mother's Day." Jewelers Circular Keystone.

"A man's search for his mother blossoms into a gift of diamonds." Costa Mesa Breeze.

"Thank you for your unique approach in motivating students to write, especially on such a positive theme." Marie Peck. Roosevelt Elementary. Anaheim, CA.

PART THREE
Resources

Resources

Following is a list of addresses that adoptees, birthparents, and/or adoptive parents may consult for further information. Some addresses may have changed since this publication.

National Search And Support Organizations

Adoptee's Liberty Movement
Association (ALMA)
P. O. Box 727 Radio City Station
New York, NY 10101-0727
212-581-1568

Adoption Crossroads
National Headquarters
401 E. 74th Street
New York, NY 10021-3919
212-988-0110

Concerned United Birthparents (CUB)
National Headquarters
2000 Walker Street
Des Moines, IA 50317
800-822-2777

Orphan Voyage
National Headquarters
2141 Road 2300
Cedaredge, CO 81413
303-856-3937

Registries

International Soundex Reunion
Registry
P.O. Box 2312
Carson City, NV 89702-2312
702-882-7755

Where to Write for Vital Records

This publication on where to inquire about birth, death, marriage and divorce records is for sale by the U. S. Government Printing Office.

Where to Write for Vital Records
U. S. Department of Health and Human
Services
Superintendent of Documents
Mail Stop: SSOP
Washington, DC 20402-9328

Birth Records and Master Death File

D. C. Vital Records
800 9th St SW 1st Floor
Washington, D. C 20024
202-783-1809

Social Welfare Organizations

Adoptee - Birthparent Searches (ABC)
234 N. 2nd St.
Jeanette, PA 15644
John Howard, Exec. Officer
(310) 285-6786

Adoptee - Birthparent Support Network (ABSN)
3421 M St. NW, No. 328
Washington, DC 20007
Robyn S. Quinter, Bd. Member
(202) 686-4611

Adoptees' Birthparents' Association
P. O. Box 33
Camarillo, CA 93011
Alberta F. Sorensen, Contact
(805) 482-8667

Adoptees and Natural Parents Organization (ANPO)
949 Lacon Drive
Newport News, VA 23608
Billie Quigley, Pres.
(804) 874-9091

Adoptees In Search (AIS)
P. O. Box 41016
Bethesda, MD 20824
Joanne W. Small MSW, Dir.
(301) 656-8555

Adoption and Family Reunion Center (AFRC)
Box 1860
Cape Coral, FL 33910
Sandra Musser, Pres.
(813) 542-1342

Adoption Identity Movement (AIM)
P. O. Box 9265
Grand Rapids, MI 49509
Peg Richer, Dir.
(616) 531-1380

Adoption Information Services (AIS)
P. O. Box 82706
Kenmore, WA 98208
Hide Iba, Treas.
(206) 325-9500

Adoptive Families Of America (AFA)
3333 Hwy. 100 N.
Minneapolis, MN 55422
Susan Freivalds, Exec. Dir.
(612) 535-4829

Advocation Legislation For Adoption Reform Movement (ALARM)
P. O. Box 1860
Cape Coral, FL 33910
Sandra Musser, Exec. Dir.
(813) 542-1342

Alma Society - Adoptees' Liberty Movement Association (ALMA)
P. O. Box 727, Radio City Sta.
New York, NY 10101-0727
Florence Anna Fisher, Founder & Pres.
(212) 581-1568

American Adoption Congress (AAC)
1000 Connecticut Ave. NW, Ste. 9
Washington, DC 20036
Kate Burke, Pres.
(202) 483-3399

American World War II Orphans Network
P. O. Box 4369
Bellingham, WA 98227
Ann Bennett Mix, Dir.
(360) 733-1678

Concerned Persons For Adoption (CPFA)
P. O. Box 179
Whippany, NJ 07981
Anna Marie O'Loughlin, Pres.
(201) 492-5921

Concerned United Birthparents (CUB)
2000 Walker St.
Des Moines, IA 50317
Janet Fenton, Pres.
(515) 263-9558

Families Adopting Children Everywhere (FACE)
P. O. Box 28058, Northwood Sta.
Baltimore, MD 21239
C. A. Tolley, Exec. Dir.
(410) 488-2656

Families For Private Adoption
P. O. Box 6375
Washington, DC 20015
Janet Droge, Pres.
(202) 722-0338

Friends In Adoption
(FIA)
P. O. Box 659
Auburn, WA 98071-0659
Debbie Allman, Pres.
(206) 343-3153

International Concerns For Children
(ICCC)
911 Cyress Dr.
Boulder, CO 80303
Anna Marie Merrill, Treas.
(303) 494-8333

International Soundex Reunion Registry
(ISRR)
P. O. Box 2312
Carson City, NV 89702-2312
Anthony S. Vilardi, Registrar
(702) 882-7755

Jewish Children's Adoption Network
(JCAN)
P. O. Box 16544
Denver, CO 80216-0544
Vicki Krausz, Exec. Dir
(303) 573-8113

Latin America Parents Association
(LAPA)
P. O. Box 339
Brooklyn NY 11234
Grayce Schulz, Pres
(718) 236-8689

Liberal Education For Adoptive Families
(LEAF)
23247 Lofton Ct. N.
Scandia, MN 55073-9753
Cheryl Hall, Dir.
(612) 433-5211

National Adoption Assistance Center
(NAAC)
2272 Colorado Blvd., No. 1228
Los Angeles, CA 90041
Joel Smith, Acting Dir.

National Adoption Center (NAC)
1500 Walnut St. Ste. 701
Philadelphia, PA 19102
Carolyn Johnson, Exec. Dir.
(215) 735-9988
(800) TO-ADOPT

National Adoption Information Clearinghouse (NAIC)
5640 Nicholson Ln., Ste. 300
Rockville, MD 20852
Debra G. Smith, Dir.
(301) 231-6512

National Coalition To End Racism In America's Child Care System
(NCERACCS)
22075 Koths
Taylor, MI 48180
Carol Coccia, Pres.
(313) 295-0257

Search and Support Groups by State

Alabama

Alabama Adoption Alliance
P. O. Box 1221
Jackson, AL 36545
205-246-3997

Arizona

Search Triad, Inc.
P. O. Box 8055
Phoenix, AZ 85066

TRIAD
7155 E. Freestone Dr.
Tucson, AZ 85730
602-7790-6320

California

San Fernando Valley Triad Search/ Support
P. O. Box 16656
North Hollywood, CA 91615
818-347-9690

Birthparent Connection
P. O. Box 230643
Encinitas, CA 92023
619-753-8288

Adoptees'/ Birthparents' Association
P. O. Box 33
Camarillo, CA 93011
805-482-8667

Adoption With Truth
66 Panoramic Way
Berkeley, CA 94704
415-704-9349

PACER of Marin
P. O. Box 826
Larkspur, CA 95154
408-356-6711

Mendo Lake Adoption Triad
620 Walnut Ave.
Ukiah, CA 95482
707-468-0648

L. A. County Adoption Search Association
P. O. Box 1461
Roseville, CA 95661
916-784-2711

Connecticut

Adoption Healing
Fairfield, CT
203-866-8988

Ties That Bind
P. O. Box 3119
Milford, CT 06460
203-874-2023

Colorado

Adoptees In Search
Contract Sta. #27, Box 323
Lakewood, CO 80215
303-232-6302

Delaware

Finders Keepers (Headquarters)
P. O. Box 748
Bear, DE 19701-0748
302-834-8888

Florida

Tallahassee Adoption Support Group
275 John Know Rd., #F-104
Tallahasse, FL 32303
904-385-8703

Mid-Florida Adoption Reunions
P. O. Box 3475
Belleview, FL 32620
904-237-1955

Organized Adoption Search Information Service
P. O. Box 53-0761
Miami Shores, FL 33153
305-757-0942

Adoptee Birthfamily Connection
P. O. Box 22363
Ft. Lauderdale, FL 33335
305-370-7100

Adoption Family and Reunion Center
P. O. Box 1860
Cape Coral, FL 33910
800-477-SEEK

Georgia

Adoptee Birthparent Connection
4565 Pond Lane
Marietta, Georgia 30144
404-642-9063

Adoption Beginnings
P. O. Box 440121
Kennesaw, GA 30144
404-590-9836

Hawaii

Adoption Circle of Hawaii
4614 Kileau Ave. # 431
Honolulu, HI 96816
808-737-7969

Idaho

Adoption Support Group
P. O. Box 2316
Ketchum, ID 83340
208-726-8543 Search Finders of Idaho
P. O. Box 7941
Boise, ID 83707
208-375-9803

Illinois

Missing Pieces
P. O. Box 7541
Springfield, IL 62791-7541
217-787-8450

Adoption Triangle
P. O. Box 384
Park Forest, IL 60466
708-481-8916

Indiana

Adoptees Identity Doorway
P. O. Box 361
South Bend, IN 46624
219-272-3520

Differences Adoption Resource
P. O. Box 187
Sharpsville, IN 46068
317-963-2835

Indiana Adoption Coalition
P. O. Box 1292
Kokomo, IN 46901
317-453-4427

Coping With Adoption
61 Country Farm Rd.
Peru, IN 46970
317-567-4139

Reunion Registry of Indiana
P.O. Box 361
South Bend, IN 46624
Betty Heide 219-272-3520
Mickey Carty 317-935-1873

Iowa

Family Search Services
P. O. Box 30106
Des Moines, IA 50310
515-255-0356

Kansas

Adoption Concerns Triangle
1427 N. Harrison
Topeka, KS 66608
913-357-1581

Wichita Adult Adoptees
4551 S. Osage
Wichita, KS 67217-4743
316-522-8772

Kentucky

Adoptee Awareness
P. O. Box 23019
Anchorage, KY 40233
502-241-6358

Louisiana

Adoption Connection of Louisiana
7301 W. Judge Perez, Suite 311
Arabi, LA 70032
504-454-7728

Adoption Triad Network, Inc.
P. O. Box 3932
Lafayette, LA 70502
318-984-3682

Maine

Adoption Search Consultants of Maine
P. O. Box 2793
S. Portland, ME 04306
207-773-3378

Adoption Support Group of Penobscot Bay
Taylor's Point
Tenant's Harbor, ME 04860
207-372-6322

Maryland

Adoptees In Search
P. O. Box 41016
Bethesda, MD 20824
301-656-8555

Massachusetts

TRY-Resource/ Referral Center
P. O. Box 989
Northampton, MA 01061-0989
413-584-6599

The Adoption Connection (TAC)
11 Peabody Square #6
Peabody, MA 01960
508-532-1261

Michigan

Adoption Identity Movement
P. O. Box 812
Hazel Park, MI 48030-0812
313-884-9222

Truth in the Adoption Triad
8107 Webster Rd.
Mt. Morris, MI 48454
313-686-3988

Bonding By Blood, Unlimited
4710 Cottrell Rd.
Vassar, MI 48768
517-823-8248

Kalamazoo Birthparent Support Group
8040 S. Westnedge #3
Kalamazoo, MI 49002
616-324-0634

Adoption Insight
P. O. Box 171
Portage, MI 49081
616-327-1999

Adoption Identity Movement
P. O. Box 9265
Grand Rapids, MI 49509
616-531-1380

Roots and Reunions
421 Cedar Street
Sault Ste. Marie, MI 49783
906-635-5922

Post Adoption Support Services
1221 Minnesota Ave.
Gladstone, MI 49837
906-428-4861

Minnesota

Minnesota Reunion Registry
23247 Lofton Ct.
N. Scandia, MN 55073-9752
612-636-7031

Mississippi

Adoption Information Network
P. O. Box 4154
Meridian, MS 39304
601-482-7556

Missouri

Support Open Adoption Records
Search/ Support Group
4589 Hopewell Rd
Wentzville, MO 63385
314-828-5726

Kansas City Adult Adoptees
P. O. Box 11828
Kansas City, MO 64138-9998
816-356-5213

Connecting Adoptees
P. O. Box 30252
Kansas City, MO 64112
816-333-5656

Nebraska

Adoption Triad Midwest
P. O. Box 37273
Omaha, NE 68137
402-895-3706

New Hampshire

Living In Search of Answers
P. O. Box 215
Gilsum, NH 03448
603-357-5218

Adoption Binding Circle
Rte. 2, Box 125
Claremont, NH 03743
603-542-6206

Circle of Hope
P. O. Box 127
Somersworth, NH 03878
603-692-6320

New Jersey

Adoption Reunion Coalition of New Jersey
15 Fir Pl.
Hazlet, NJ 07730
908-739-9385

Adoptive Parents for Open Records
P. O. Box 193
Long Valley, NJ 07853
908-850-1706

Origins
P. O. Box 556
Whippany, NJ 07981
201-428-9683

Adoption Support Network, Inc.
505 West Hamilton Ave., #207
Linwood, NJ 08221
609-653-4242

Adoption Support Group of Central New Jersey
500 4-B Auten Rd
Somerville, NJ 08876
908-874-8983

New York

Birthparent Support Network (Headquarters)
P. O. Box 120
N. White Plains, NY 10603
914-682-2250

Candid Adoption Talk
175-A Fawn Hill Rd.
Tuxedo, NY 10987
914-351-4522

Adoption Connection
P. O. Box 492
Northville, NY 12134
518-863-6793

Triangle of Truth
P. O. Box 2039
Liverpool, NY 13089
315-622-0620

B.U.S.S.
P. O. Box 299
Victor, NY 14564
716-763-4777

Jamestown Adoption Triad
3760 Cowing Rd.
Lakewood, NY 14750
716-763-4777

Bloodroots
620 Central Chapel Rd.
Brooktondale, NY 14817
607-539-7401

North Carolina

Carolina Adoption Triangle Support
116 West Queen St.
Hillsborough, NC
916-732-2751

Adoption Information Exchange
P. O. Box 1917
Matthews, NC 28106
704-846-8025

Ohio

Adoption Triangle Unity
4144 Packard Rd.
Toledo, OH 43613
419-244-7072

Adoptees' Search Rights
P. O. Box 8713
Toledo, OH 43613
419-691-3463

Adoption Network
302 Overlook Park Dr.
Cleveland, OH 44110
216-481-7019

Sunshine Reunions
1175 Virginia Ave.
Akron, OH 44306
216-773-4691

Chosen Children
311 Springbrook
Dayton, OH 45405
513-274-8017

Oklahoma

Shared Heartbeats
P. O. Box 12125
Oklahoma City, OK 73157
405-722-BOND

Oklahoma Adoption Triad
P. O. Box 2503
Broken Arrow, OK 74013

Oregon

ALARM Network
9203 S.W. Cree Circle
Tualatin, OR 97062
503-235-3669

Family Ties
4537 Souza St.
Eugene, OR 97402
503-461-0752

South Oregon Adoptive Rights
P. O. Box 202
Grants Pass, OR 97526
503-479-3143

Pennsylvania

Pittsburgh Adoption Lifeline
P. O. Box 52
Gibsonia, PA 15044

Pittsburgh Adoption Connection
P. O. Box 4564
Pittsburgh, PA 15205
412-279-2511

Adoption Forum
(Headquarters)
525 S. 4th St., Suite 3465
Philadelphia, PA 19147
215-238-1116

South Carolina

Adoptees and Birthparents in Search
P. O. Box 5551
West Columbia, SC 29171
803-224-8020

Tennessee

Group for Openness in Adoption
518 General G. Partton Rd.
Nashville, TN 37221
615-646-8116

Roots
7110 Westway Center
Knoxville, TN 37919
615-691-7412

Right to Know
P. O. Box 34334
Bartlett, TN 38134
901-386-2197

Texas

Searchline of Texas
1516 Old Orchard Rd.
Irving, TX 75061
214-445-7005

Adoption Knowledge Affiliates
P. O. Box 402033
Austin, TX 78704
512-442-8252

Adoptees, Adopt/Birth Parents
In Search
4206 Roxbury
El Paso, TX, 79922
915-581-0478

Utah

Adoption Connection of Utah
1349 Mariposa Ave.
Salt Lake City, UT 84106
801-278-4858

Vermont

Central Vermont Adoption Support Group
Rte. 1, Box 83
East Calais, VT 05650
802-456-8850

Adoption Alliance of Vermont
91 Court St.
Middlebury, VT 05753
802-388-7569

Virginia

Adoptees Support For Birthmothers
8630 Granby St.
Norfolk, VA 23503
804-480-1571

Adoptees and Natural Parents
949 Lacon Dr.
Newport News, VA 23602
804-874-9091

Adult Adoptees In Search
P. O. Box 203
Ferrum, VA 24088
703-365-0712

Washington

Adoption Search/Reconciliation
14320 S. E. 170th St.
Renton, WA 98058
206-228-6179

Washington Adoption Rights Movement
5950 6th Ave. S., #107
Seattle, WA 98107-3317
206-767-9510

Touched By Adoption
205 Brock Str., #7
Walla Walla, WA 99362
509-529-7217

Wisconsin

Adoption Information and Direction
P. O. Box 23764
Milwaukee, WI 53224
414-233-6487

Adoption Resource Network
P. O. Box 174
Coon Valley, WI 54623-0174
608-452-3146

Adoption Resource Network
P. O. Box 8221
Eau Claire, WI 54702-8221
715-835-6695

Canadian Agencies

Adoption Council of Ontario
1545 Narva Rd.
Mississauga, Ontario L5H 3H4
416-482-0021

Magazines

AdoptNet
P. O. Box 50514
Palo Alto, CA 94303-0514
415-949-4730

Reunions- The Magazine
P. O. Box 11727
Milwaukee, WI 53211
414-263-4567

People Searching News
P. O. Box 22611
Fort Lauderdale, FL 33335-2611

Search And Support Referral

American Adoption Congress (AAC)
1000 Connecticut Avenue, NW
Suite 9
Washington, D.C. 20036
800-274-OPEN

Independent Search Consultants (ISC)
P. O. Box 10192
Costa Mesa, CA 92627

Council on Equal Rights in Adoption
(CERA)
401 East 74th Street, Suite 17-D
New York, NY 10021
212-988-0110

U.S. Government Agencies

Immigration and Naturalization Services
(INS)
U.S. Department of Justice
425 I Street NW
Washington, DC 30536
202-514-2000

The National Archives
Washington, DC 20408
202-501-5402

Passport Records
Department of State, Passport Agency
1425 K Street NW
Washington, DC 20524
202-647-0518

Social Security Administration
6401 Security Boulevard
Baltimore, MD 21235
410-965-8882

Child Welfare League of America
(CWLA)
440 First St. NW. Suite 310
Washington, D.C. 20402
202-638-2952

Following are some of the books purchased by the Orange County Public Library in California from the proceeds of the Why Mom Deserves A Diamond anthology booklets. As of this publication, over $6,700 has been donated for books on creative writing, self expression, and for adoptees who are searching for their origins.

1997 Contest

Jewelry by Artists in Italy 1945-1995, Awakening the Poet Within, Writer's Web: Get Online and Get Published, The Atlas of Languages, How To Write and Sell Historical Fiction, The Insider's Guide to Writing for Screen and Television, The Complete Idiot's Guide to Creative Writing, How to Adopt Internationally, Everything You Need to Know to Write, Publish, and Sell Your Book, Confessions of a Lost Mother, The Woman Who Spilled Words All over Herself, and Naked in Cyberspace.

1996 Contest

Susan Avallone editor, "Film Writer's Guide", Ann Copeland, "ABC's of Writing Fiction", William Higginson, "Haiku Handbook", William Zinsser, "Writing to Learn", "How to Write What you Want and Sell What you Write", Frieda Gates, How to Write, Illustrate and Design Children's Books", Cherry Kelly, "Writing the World," Eugene Ferraro, "You Can Find Anyone", Betty Jean Lifton, "Lost and Found and "Twice Born."

1995 Contest

Herbert Engel, "Handbook of Creative Learning Exercises." Mary Austin, "Writing thc Western Landscape." "Oxford Companion to Women's Writing in the US." Rebecca Carroll, "I Know what thc Red Clay Looks Like." Ruth Heller. "Cache of Jewels." Jeremy Marshall. "Question of English." Mordecai Brill. "Write Your Own Wedding." Gilbert Norris. "How to Write & Sell a Christian Novel." Stephen Gladis. "Write, Type: Personality Types & Writing." Dave Kemper. Writer's Express." Dick Weisman. "Creating Melodies." Beginning Writer's Thesaurus. Don McKinney, "Magazine Writing That Sells." Rod Hansen, "You've Got To Read This." And Howe. "Playing With Words."

1994 Contest

"Into the Deep- A Writer's Look at Creativity"; Susan Cahill, "Writing Women's Lives;" Michael Bugeja, "The Art and Craft of Poetry;" "Writer's Digest Guide to Good Writing;" James Frey: "How to Write a Damn Good Novel ll;" Jack Hodgins, "Passion for Narrative;" Donald Newlove, "Invented Voices (Inspired Dialogue for Writers and Readers)," Albert Zuckerman, "Writing the Blockbuster Novel", Susan Artof; "Writing for Pleasure", Robert A. Day; "How to Write and Publish a Scientific Paper", and Anita Jesse, "Let the Part Play You, 3rd ed."

Bibliography

Aigner, Hai J. *Faint Trails*. Paradigm Press. 1980.

Brodzinsky, Schecter & Henig. *Being Adopted - The Lifelong Search for Self.* Doubleday. New York. 1992.

Burgess, Linda Cannon. *The Art of Adoption.* Acropolis Books Ltd. 1976.

Clewer, Lisa. *Official ALMA Searcher's Guide for Adults.* 1982. Printed and distributed by Adoptee's Liberty Movement Association.

Culligan, Joseph J. *You, Too, Can Find Anybody. A Reference Manual.* Hallmark Press, Inc. 1993.

-------. *Adoption Searches Made Easier.* FJA, Inc. Miami, FL. 1996.

Fisher, Florence. *The Search for Anna Fisher.* Fawcett Crest. 1973.

Gediman, Judith, and Brown,Linda P. *Birth Bond, Reunions Between Birthparents & Adoptees... What Happens After.* 1989. New Horizon Press.

Floyd County Chamber of Commerce of New Albany Economics Development Commission. *A Profile of New Albany and Floyd County, Indiana.* 1985.

Gohman, James. Floyd County Historical Society. Special Committee. 1994

Gravelle, Karen, and Fischer, Susan. *Where Are My Birth Parents?* Walker and Company. NY. 1993.

Leitch, David. *Family Secrets. A Writer's Search to Find His Past.* Delecorte Press. 1984.

Lifton, Betty Jean. *Twice Born.* McGraw Hill. 1975.

-------. *Lost and Found*: The Adoption experience. New York. Harper and Row. 1988.

-------. *Journey of the Adopted Self.* Basicbooks. New York. 1994.

Melina. Lois Ruskai. *Making Sense of Adoption.* Harper And Row. 1989.

Paul, Ellen. *Adoption Choices. A guidebook to National and International Adoption Resources.* Visible Ink Press. Detroit, MI. 1991.

Roles, Patricia. *Saying Good-bye to a Baby. Volume 2-A. A counselor's Guide to Birthparent Loss and Grief in Adoption.* Child Welfare League of America. Washington D.C. 1989.

Sachdev, Paul. *Unlocking the Adoption Files.* Lexington Books. 1989.

Sorosky, Arthur D, Annette Baran, and Rueben Pannor. *The Adoption Triangle.* New York. Anchor Press. 1987.

Strauss, Jean A. *Birthright. The Guide to Search and Reunion for Adoptees, Birthparents, and Adoptive Parents.* Penguin Books. 1994.

Tribune, New Albany. Harvest Homecoming Edition. October, 1981. Pg. 4-A.

Verrier, Nancy Newton. *The Primal Wound.* Gateway Press, Inc. Baltimore, MD. 1993.

Watson, Michael. *Why Mom Deserves A Diamond.* Anthology booklets. Gallery of Diamonds Publishing. Costa Mesa, CA. 1993-1997.

Index

A

adolescent 31, 57, 87, 95, 125, 131, 133, 155
adopted angel 15
adoptive parent 6-8, 16, 27, 37-38, 49, 54, 77, 81-82, 122, 132, 135-138, 197, 203, 210
adoptive triangle 6
Africa 172
alcoholic 27, 91
Alice 150-151
ALMA 50, 55, 95-96, 197-198, 209
amended 5, 97
amendment 121
American Bank 76
amulet 38, 43, 175
ancestral bewilderment 6
ancestry 5, 8, 80
ancient lock 133
ancient voyager 5, 159
anthology booklet 172-173, 207, 210
archeologist 139
attorney 8, 25, 83
Aunt Arlie 54

B

Baptist 131, 192
bastard 27
Bible 29, 40, 53
Big Bertha 46
biological fabric 5
biological family 8, 128, 137, 143, 146, 152, 155
biological father 143, 151, 153
biological ignorance 118
biological mother 98, 134, 144, 154, 171
biological parents 6-7, 97, 101
biological relative 50, 125, 138, 157
biological reunion 73
birth certificate 5-6, 24, 96-97, 154-156, 159
birth father 137
birthday 46, 53, 80, 138, 144, 148, 154
birthmother 8, 24, 26-27, 37-41, 49-50, 53, 55-56, 67, 73, 76-77, 80-82, 86-89, 91-92, 94-97, 109, 117-119, 121, 123, 125-129, 132-133, 136-137, 139-141, 143, 146, 153-154, 156-157, 174, 194, 205
birthright 7
Biscayne 34
Biscuit 34
Black Hole 129, 134-135, 186
Blacksberry 144
blood pressure 103
blood roots 5, 99, 118
blue chairs 66
Bob 138
boogie man 95

C

Camaro 58, 66, 81, 89
cancer 28, 55
candied apples 51
Carmel 85
Carmen 3, 111
Carr, Sheila 79, 81, 93
certificate of death 154
Certificate of Live Birth 155
Chamber of Commerce 52, 209
Child Welfare Division 83, 97
chocolate 46, 51
Chosen One 32, 96
Christ 29
Christian 125, 131, 179, 207
cider 51
cigarette 17, 30, 32, 79
city county building 40, 56, 81, 122
Civilian Conservation Corps 17
Class of '80 63
Clayton, Randy 126, 130
Clemmons, Margaret 79, 94
Clowns 51
Coates, Henry 130
Coatesville 125, 127-128, 131-132, 136-137, 139, 141, 145, 147
coffin 57
Colorado 108, 199-200
Commonwealth of Massachusetts 154
Community Hospital 24, 26, 54, 68, 81, 122, 134, 155
Corinthians Thirteen 29, 102
corpse 57
cosmic coordinates 160
Costa Mesa 1-2, 108-109, 114, 179, 182, 189, 192-194, 206, 210
Country Club Plaza 100

court summary 82, 85-88, 90, 93-97, 110, 117, 119, 122, 124, 130, 133, 136, 138
Crandall, Jason 107
curtain 33, 35, 39, 79, 82, 89, 90

D

Dallas 42-43
Daniel 3-4, 180
Danville 131
Dead Sea Scrolls 128
death 19, 28, 31, 46, 57-58, 60, 72-73, 106, 122, 127, 129, 134, 136, 152, 154
Decree of Adoption 25
Destiny of Things 58
detective 67, 121
diabetes 55, 103
diamonds 64, 79-80, 113-115, 160, 172-174, 176, 179, 184, 186, 194, 210
divorce 84, 91, 94, 96, 102-103, 130, 197
DNA 134
DuPont 17, 28

E

Earth-Time 72, 152
earthquakes 118
Easter tulips 58
Ellen 4, 99, 101, 103, 108, 190, 209
emphysema 103, 148
epilepsy 103
Ewing, J.R. 42

F

Fairmont 22, 185
family hierarchy 146
family tree 5
FATHER OF CHILD 83
Featheringill Road 58, 72, 134
Fillmore 131
fire tower 72
fires 118
Fisher, Florence 50
Flood of 1937 131
floods 118
Flora, Margy 118
Frisch's Big Boy 34

G

Gallery of Diamonds 113-114, 160, 172-174, 184, 210
gemstones 172-173
genealogical exploration 127
glass blowers 51
Golden State 105
Good Friday 131
Gram negative septicemia 154
Grandfather 41, 125, 128-129, 132, 136, 144
Grandmother 125, 127, 132-133, 135-137, 139, 141-147, 156
Grantline Road 20, 22, 33, 54, 57, 67, 83, 109, 132
Great Depression 17
Great Search 133
Gremlin 64
Grimes 25, 75, 84
Guatemalan girl 111
guitar 32-33, 45-46, 63-65, 75

H

Hainlen, Randy G. 156
half-brother 83, 85, 89, 91, 96, 119
Hamilton county 86
handwriting 25, 125
Harvest Homecoming 51-52, 210
Haunted House 52
Health and Human Services 122, 197
heart disease 103
Hepatic encephalopathy 154
heredity 7, 103
heritage 8, 81, 122, 131, 146, 157
Higgins, Tommy 33-34, 45, 71
high school 17, 31-32, 51, 61, 66, 87, 90, 97, 131, 145, 172, 175-176, 178, 180, 182
highway 39, 58, 112, 125
hoax 124, 142
holy book 29
Hopkinsville 71
human creation 109

I

illegitimate 27, 83
illusions of grandeur 133
incest 27
independent search consultant 122, 206
Indiana Adoption History Registration 121
Indiana courthouses 124
Indiana State Department of Health 96, 155
Indianapolis 15, 24, 26, 39, 40-41, 54
Indianapolis 500 52
Indianapolis Star 98

internet 126
investigator 67, 129
itinerary of the universe 73

J

Jack's lunch house 29
Jenkins, Jesse 33
jewelry 64-65, 79, 93, 101-102, 104-105
Jewish 37, 54, 199
Judge Jameson 40, 49, 81, 123, 143
junior high 26, 30-31, 65, 103, 178

K

Kansas 100, 104, 108, 111, 201, 203
Kenny Ray 3, 138, 145, 157
Kentucky 16, 49, 100, 111, 144, 202
Kentucky Derby 49
Ketchersid, Margaret 176
Kircher, Scott 175
Kiwanis 51
Knobs 34, 45, 57, 72
Kokomo 156, 201
Koran 54
Krison's 102, 105, 107

L

Labor Day 141
Laguna Beach 115, 192
legislators 122
life-force 25
Lizard Boy 18
Los Angeles 104, 106-107, 174, 199
Louisville 16, 28, 34, 100

M

maiden name 49, 85-86, 91, 96-97, 123, 125-126, 129, 153
marigolds 53, 75
marijuana 30, 65
Marion County Probate Court 98, 155
marriage license 85, 123, 129, 138
marriage license application 123, 129
Martin, Greg 33
Mary Jane 3, 138, 142, 144-145, 156
Massachusetts 136, 143, 154, 202
Master Death file 127, 197
maturing 26
medical records 55
Mediterranean 54, 137
Methodist 16, 19, 53, 75, 131
Michaela 3, 160
microfilm 87
microscopic self 73
Miguel 109
minister 19, 151
Missouri 99, 102, 203
MOTHER OF CHILD 84, 119
Mother's Day 3, 53, 75, 171-172, 191-192, 194
Mozambique 172
Murphy, Hattie 125
Murphy, James 144
music 22-23, 32-33, 63, 71, 99, 102, 104, 113
musician 45, 64, 104
Muslim 54
Mustang 61, 105, 108, 109

N

nationality 37, 76, 80, 82, 103, 137
New Albany 16, 42, 43, 51, 73, 81, 99
Noblesville 84-85, 87, 89-91, 94, 97-98, 117, 123, 125
Noblesville Daily Topics 94, 98
Noblesville High School 87, 90, 97
North Delaware 26, 37, 39, 43, 56, 121, 129
nurse 148, 150-151, 180

O

obituary 130
Ohio River 16
Orange County 3, 108, 173-174, 194, 207
Orange County Newschannel 173
Orange County Public Library 3, 173
origin 3, 7-8, 37, 47, 81, 109, 117, 203, 207
Overland Park 99, 101, 108

P

Pacific Ocean 115
Panama Jack 68
Patricia 3, 209
Pennsylvania Railroad 131
Petition for Custody of Child 25, 156
pillar of salt 82
Pilot Rock 71-73, 82
Plymouth 84, 91-92, 96, 117-118
pneumonia 148
polygraph 65-69
postcard 25, 54-55, 68, 122
Price, Betty 25, 26, 40-41, 54, 67, 84, 89, 95, 96, 118-119, 129, 134, 138, 154, 156

Price, Debra Kay 156
Price, Floyd 84-87, 89, 91, 96, 123-124, 134
Price, Michael David 84, 90, 96, 135
primal Mother 73
Primitive Baptist 131
Probate court 8
Probate Judge 40
psychological journey 7
psychopath 134
publicity 95
pumpkins 52
Putnam County 124

Q

Quincy 136, 143

R

Ralph's barber shop 28
rape 27
Raymond, Jonathan 143, 155
religion 53, 131
relinquish 6, 82
Relinquished One 96
reunion 6, 7, 8, 12, 50, 73, 118, 141, 144, 146-147, 152, 157, 159, 174, 197-204, 206, 209-210
riots 118
Roger 79

S

Santa Ana 109, 114, 179, 180, 188, 193
sapphire 172-174, 177-178, 180-192, 194
scarlet "A" 25
Scarly, Hank 100, 102
scientific curiosity 142
Sears Silvertone 63
second birth 6
secrets 4, 82, 95, 138, 209
sex 144
Shalaars 63-64, 66, 69, 80, 90, 94, 99, 102, 106
Slavo 63
social worker 8, 77, 98, 138, 159
South Coast Plaza 108, 111
spelling contest 32
spider 20, 22, 56, 89
spiritual awakening 72
Spring Street 34
Starrdust 33, 52
stillborn 135, 143
Stewart, Betty 124, 126, 129
Stewart, Hattie 127, 134, 137, 141
Stewart, Otis 125, 127, 130, 132
Sullivan, Ernie 94
survivor 27, 129
Suzie 3, 138, 139, 144, 157

T

tobacco 104, 148
tornado 131
Tornado of 1917 131
Tregger 63
tuberculosis 103
Turner, Dr. William 25, 155
twelve roses 75
Twilight Zone 39

U

Uncle Elmo 60
Uncle Henry 54
Utah 108, 205

V

Vital Records Division 96-97

W

Watson, Martha 83, 97, 146, 156
Watson, Stoy 3, 97, 151, 155
Walsh, Veronica 109
West Milton 130
White Horse Inn 88, 89, 107
whore 27
Why Mom Deserves a Diamond 2, 12, 144, 171-172, 174, 194, 207, 210
Wilcox, Hazel 83, 97
womb 5, 53, 71, 73,
Woody's 32
Wyle E. Coyote 30

X

X and Y axis 109

Y

yearbook 30, 87, 97

Z

zebra swallowtails 20
Zemartans 66

Order Form

In Search of Mom .... $19.95 plus $3.50 P/H
Journey Of An Adoptee. **Please send me ____ copies**

The following booklets contain the most outstanding Mother's Day essays written by Orange County, California students, grades two through twelve, that were selected from over 18,000 entries. These heartwarming booklets will render many years of enjoyment in discovering how these students expressed their appreciation for their mothers.

Why Mom Deserves A Diamond .... $24.95 plus $3.50 P/H
1,500 Winners. 1998. **Please send me ____ copies**
Why Mom Deserves A Diamond .... $21.95 plus $3.50 P/H
1,002 Winners. 1997. 64 pgs. **Please send me ____ copies**
Why Mom Deserves A Diamond .... $18.95 plus $3.50 P/H
732 Winners. 1996. 56 pgs. **Please send me ____ copies**
Why Mom Deserves A Diamond .... $13.95 plus $3.00 P/H
391 Winners. 1995. 41 pgs. **Please send me ____ copies**
Why Mom Deserves A Diamond .... $12.95 plus $2.50 P/H
1994. 28 pgs. **Please send me ____ copies**
Why Mom Deserves A Diamond .... $7.00 plus $2.00 P/H
1993. 15 pgs. **Please send me ____ copies**

California residents add 7.75% sales tax.
Please Print Clearly

Name ____

Address ____

City __________________ Street _____________ Zip _____

Phone (   ) _____________________

Please send check or money order to: **Gallery Of Diamonds, 2915 Redhill Ave., Ste. #G-102, Costa Mesa, CA 92626. Or call 1-800-667-4440.** Books will be sent in 2-3 weeks.

Credit Card (check one) M/C __ Visa __ AmerExpress __

Credit Card # ___________________________ Exp. _______